NO PROPER GRIEF

A JOURNEY OF LOSS & RESILIENCE

By Jakob Franzen

Published by
Hybrid Global Publishing
301 E 57th Street
4th Floor
New York, NY 10022

Manufactured in the United States of America, or in the United Kingdom when distributed elsewhere.

Franzen, Jakob.
No Proper Grief: A Journey of Loss & Resilience
    ISBN: 978-1-957013-11-4
    eBook: 978-1-957013-12-1
    LCCN: 2021925579

Cover design by: Jonathan Pleska
Copyediting by: Virginia Earl
Interior design by: Suba Murugan
Author photo by: Errich Petersen

Contents

To Jayson,

During our entire life together, you continually reminded me that I was enough.

Now, this has made all the difference.

1

Goodbye

The afternoon was painted in a shade of hopelessness. Our family had gone home to rest, and the last visiting friend had just left me. It was so good to see her. She had come into my life as part of the package with my husband. She was one of the people he was most excited for me to meet when we started dating.

This afternoon had just been the two of us while he lay quietly sleeping in the hospital bed. We poured over the question that had been asked a thousand times, the question that had been on the lips of everyone who had entered that room, the question that seared itself across my heart, "Why?" Neither of us had an answer, only tears. I usually prefer emotional distance even with my friends, but her hug was one of the longest and best I had felt in a while. It was filled with compassion, love, and all the strength she could try to give me. I missed her when she left.

I sat in the vinyl recliner next to the window. It was a chair only hospitals could have. It was a hideous pea soup green with wheels on the bottom. After years of use, it yielded to the reclining position far too quickly and made it difficult to sit upright. I pulled my legs up into the chair and wrapped a blanket around me as I stared out the window.

It was a typical January day in Texas with low clouds and only the suggestion of winter lingering in the air. The hospital looked far different than it had when I worked there years ago. The room we were in would have looked out over the front drive of the hospital at that time. Now, it looked out over a new outpatient building with valet parking. It struck me at that moment that I had paid for parking— I had paid to sit with my husband as he died—one of the many ironies of an institution that is in the business of compassion.

As I sat there, holding the blanket close and looking down on the pebbled roof of the porte-cochère below, I thought about what a long week it had been — and how unexpected. Even as the inevitable unfolded, I resisted. I somehow thought that if I fought against it, if I denied it, things would be different. They were not. This part of the nightmare had begun on a Wednesday night.

I had gotten our daughters bathed and put to bed, and Jayson and I were in our bed watching TV. We kept up with several series, and it had become somewhat of a ritual in our relationship to share time in the evenings watching them and discussing what we thought. Although lately he had begun to lose interest in them, little did I know then that I'd end up watching the series finales of them alone. As the days went by, it became more and more difficult for him to get comfortable.

The disease processes in his body had caused edema in his legs, and a scratch on one of his calves would not heal. He had to be on oxygen all of the time now. The oxygen equipment that was paid for by our insurance made life difficult. The home unit had to be in the closet with a 100ft tube running to the bed because it was large and sounded like a tractor when it was running. The portable concentrator was hardly portable. It required a dolly to be carried around because it weighed almost10 pounds. Using any kind of carrying strap was out of the question given his condition. So, we bought our own home and portable units. They were both lighter, quieter, and much more convenient. The new portable unit gave him a much higher quality of life.

That night he was incredibly restless and didn't want to keep me awake. I assured him that I was tired enough that I would never notice, but he insisted on going to the TV room across the house where he could watch some TV and fall asleep on the couch. I offered to help him, but he refused. "No," he said in a clear and agitated voice. If there is one thing that never changed about my husband during this was his independent streak. He never wanted to be or even appear to be helpless.

As I walked back toward the bed, I heard a noise. I turned around instantly and saw him lying in the doorway of our bedroom. He had lost his balance and fallen. I rushed to him, terrified when I saw some blood on his lip. I helped him sit up and made sure that nothing was broken or that nothing needed stitches. I told him to stay put while I got a wet cloth to clean him up a little and see if he needed a bandage on his hand. He nodded, and I went into the bathroom to get a washcloth. When I returned, he was gone. He had, of course, gotten himself up and already made it into the TV room. I don't know that I have ever felt both that angry and sad at the same time.

I was so sorry that he was losing his ability to walk around and navigate on his own. I was mad that his stubborn streak wouldn't let me do what comes naturally to me — care for him. I was immediately overcome with guilt at my anger. How could I be so angry at someone I loved so much and who was in so much pain? I felt ashamed. I went to him and offered to clean him up, but he refused. He was already on the couch and told me in no uncertain terms he was fine and to let him be. I went to bed, my cheeks hot with tears.

I didn't sleep well. But that was nothing new. I hadn't had a good night's sleep since the attack from this disease began. It had come out of nowhere — or at least it seemed so to me. We had returned from our annual trip to Cancun. Life was in upheaval because we were building a new house. It was to be our dream home. We got to design much of it to be just the way we wanted, and we used every lesson we had learned from the houses we had owned together and even the ones that we had owned apart. As timing often goes when one is building and selling, the processes rarely align.

We had sold our previous home, and we were in an apartment near our neighborhood. We had taken a couple of extra hours to decide whether or not to lease. So we lost the ground floor apartment, and the apartment we ended up with was on the third floor. A fact that would become more and more a challenge as this disease progressed. The day after we got home from our trip, Jayson woke up with swollen legs. I had never seen his legs that way. They were so swollen he couldn't even get his shoes on by himself, much less tie them. We wondered if it had anything to do with spending so much time in an airplane the day before. But as he had often told me, just because two things happen simultaneously does not mean they are related, and indeed these were not.

The swelling would come and go over the next year. Visits to our doctor turned into visits to a gastroenterologist, a hepatologist, a pulmonologist, and a rheumatologist. I would come to know far more about these fields than I ever cared to know. Whatever was attacking his liver and causing scar tissue was also attacking his lungs and causing scar tissue there. I will never forget my disbelief when he had to go on oxygen. It seemed so sudden. It broke my heart to see one of the strongest men I knew suddenly hobbled by something neither of us could control. These symptoms continued to get slowly and progressively worse over the next year. The worry in my heart grew in proportion, as did fear. I was terrified to lose my husband. The flashes of a life without him created a sense of panic that would manifest itself as a form of irritability that I had to control.

When I got up to get our daughters ready for school that Thursday morning, I went to the TV room to check on him. The alarm was going off on his concentrator. I quietly checked the tubing and adjusted his cannula. Once things were back in order, I went to wake up the girls for breakfast. For them, it was a typical morning.

I tried so hard to give them as much normalcy as possible during so many life changes. They were settling into our new home — we had been there 9 months now.

Waffles remained a favorite for breakfast, and I was happy to oblige. I had just left a job and was waiting on a new one to start. So I had time to indulge my girls in breakfast requests. I got them dressed and ready to go, and we went downstairs to the TV room so they could kiss their Daddy goodbye. The alarm was going off again on his concentrator.

Hence, as I readjusted things, he awoke highly agitated and began yelling for us to leave him alone. I'll never forget the look of fear on my daughters' faces. They had never seen him this way. I was able to get him calmed enough to kiss them. He loved them beyond words, and that always trumped everything in the end. As I drove them to school, we talked about how when you're sick, you can get irritable even with the ones you love the most. At 5 and 7, they did their best to understand. I didn't tell them how much I understood that morning, nor did I tell them how much I didn't want to believe was true.

The look I had seen in his eye was one of confusion when he woke up. It was a look that conveyed his current state. I would have thought him hypoxic from the oxygen tubing getting crimped in the night, but I knew better. I knew as I returned home that something had shifted and that I would need to make some decisions about his care because I was no longer sure what needed to be done. For the moment, I let him rest. I had decided to complete some professional development while I was between jobs, and I used this as a distraction. However, it had become more complex and more challenging for me to distract myself those days. The reality of the situation was always just a pause away.

I worked up my courage after lunch to try to talk him into going back to the bedroom so that he could lay in the bed. I felt sure that I could make him more comfortable there. I walked to the couch where he was sleeping and knelt down beside it. Even sleeping, he looked tired. He had been fighting this thing for a long time, and it was taking a heavy toll. I placed my hand gently on his shoulder and whispered, "Can I help you to the bed?" His eyes fluttered open, and he gratefully nodded. I helped him slowly sit up and then gently raised him to his feet. I had always been taller and bigger than him, and at that moment, I was glad. I was able to support him and steady him with little effort. He held on to me with confidence. Lifting him into the bed wasn't hard, but I could tell it bothered him. He was so independent, and the fact that I had to help him to bed bothered him deeply. I tried to make as little of it as possible, and though bothered, I could tell he was grateful as I fussed with the pillows to make him as comfortable as possible. With the TV on, he spent the afternoon dozing, and I sat with my worry.

If there is one thing we know how to do in the south, it is to show our love with food. Jayson worked with some of the most amazing people I have ever met. You would expect those who work in neonatology to have a high sense of compassion. Still, the friends he worked with had compassion to spare, and it spilled beyond the neonates and flowed directly to one of their own when he needed them. In their generosity, they had set up a food delivery schedule when Jayson had gone on disability to help out while I focused on his care. We were never without a hot meal, whether home-cooked or sourced from a favorite restaurant. I was humbled every day by this act of pure kindness. I hadn't asked for it — my pride wouldn't have allowed it. They just did it to take care of us by turning compassion into action.

On this particular evening, the food was coming from one of the neonatologists. He sent me a text when he was on the way, asking if Jayson would be up to talking with him. I told him I'd check and see because he had been sleeping. When I went into the bedroom, I smiled and asked Jayson if he wanted to see him thinking he'd be overjoyed to say hello. This particular physician was one Jayson had worked closely with and had grown to enjoy sharing shifts. To my surprise, he replied with a forceful, "No!" I pressed him. "Why not? He'd love to see you."

"Tell him I'm sleeping. I can't let him see me this way. Please tell him I'm sleeping!" The pleading in his voice reminded me that I was not the only one dealing with pride in this situation. He couldn't bear to be seen weak or compromised. I understood. As much as I didn't like his answer and thought that he could do with seeing a friendly face that wasn't mine, I understood. It had been hard enough for him to work using an oxygen concentrator and his co-workers to see him in that condition. The last thing he wanted was for anyone to see him in the bed and unable to get up.

About that time, the doorbell rang, and I knew I'd have to make excuses, but somewhere in the back of my mind I knew the situation had pushed me to the edge. Bubbling to the surface was the horrifying fact that I could no longer control this. Not the disease, of course, but everything surrounding it. I was forever the consummate planner. My role in our relationship had been to keep all the trains running on time. I planned the trips, created the itineraries, booked the flights, and told everyone where to be for maximum ease. I was buckling under the weight of what was before me, and my steps were weighted and measured. I was panicking. I had to collect my composure and be gracious. I took a deep breath, smiled, and opened the door.

Food. His arms were filled with bags and containers of food. There is something about seeing a gifted physician engaged in the mundane that gives you a moment, no matter how brief, to celebrate being human. No matter how advanced our knowledge, at our core we're all human — bound together by life's mundane tasks like juggling food to deliver to friends. We are connected by the everyday and by the qualities we share. Life itself is one of those things that undeniably binds us together as human beings. I grabbed a bag from his full hands and invited him in. As we walked to the kitchen and sat the food down on the island, he asked, "Is he okay seeing me?"

I had prepared what I was going to say. I had quickly rehearsed it in my head the perfect response that wouldn't offend. After all, I was always the one to say the right thing. I was the one who could ease disappointment and disarm even the most contentious of comments. I sat the bag I had been holding down, and I turned to him, ready to deliver my line. It unraveled. The thread of my well-woven response unwound quickly and immediately. I looked him in the eye and felt the burning heat in my eyes and the involuntary contorting of my face that comes from weeping. It was less than a second before tears were running down my cheeks, and the well-prepared line that was ready to be delivered by the voice that had won 100 speaking awards crumbled into a sad, quaking, whimpering, "No." That quiet and low "no" was followed by what had been bubbling just beneath the surface all day. A cry for help that I had been too proud to utter came spilling out of my mouth before I could stop it. "I don't know what to do!"

He hugged me. I usually wouldn't have let that happen. Especially with someone I only really knew by reputation. But there is a specific power in compassion that undercuts pride and emotional defenses. He made no immediate jump to asking me what was wrong—no quick jump to end that moment. There we were in the present, and all I could say was that I was sorry for breaking down. All I could say was that I was sorry for losing my composure. What I know now that I didn't realize then was that I was apologizing for being human. I was letting my shame of not being able to handle the situation get the better of me. After all, I was always the one who took care of others. I was always the one who could find a way out of the problems. I was always the one who could find a way to make things better. But suddenly, I was not that person, and for some reason, that was manifesting itself as my own failing.

As I collected myself, he asked how he could help. No judgment, just help. We stood in my kitchen and talked for a while. I was struggling with honoring Jayson's wishes of not wanting to go to the hospital and with doing the right thing for him. After all, if he could be helped and I didn't take him, I wouldn't be able to forgive myself. As fate would have it, this particular neonatologist who visited on this specific day had exactly the personal experience I needed to hear. He had been in a similar situation with a family member.

He shared his story about how he handled it and why he made the decision that he had made. There is a specific power in stories. He didn't stand there and tell me what I should do — he never gave me one moment of instruction. Instead, his story gave me something to hold on to. It gave me a model I could try on for myself. I could see myself in his story. I could see what I would do that was the same and what I would do differently. His story gave me power — a power to do what I needed to do. The story had arrived at just the right time.

That night Jayson wasn't feeling any better and he stayed in bed. I brought him a small plate of food, but he couldn't eat much of it. After I had our daughters bathed and set to play a little before I tucked them in, I sat down and talked to him. I told him how much I thought getting him to the hospital would be beneficial. I told him that I felt like I was at the end of my ability to care for him. He resisted. The same pride that I had seen surface when I had to lift him into bed was back. He didn't want the people he worked with to see him hospitalized. He couldn't bear for them to know he had lost his ability to function. We arrived at a compromise that if he had to be taken to the hospital, I would take him to a different hospital's main campus, where he didn't work. That way he'd be able to get excellent care and be out of his colleagues' sight. At that moment, it was the best that I could do.

Pride is a dangerous enemy of vulnerability. It seeks to place us in a position of being in our best condition. Frequently, it becomes a veneer over our challenges and struggles. My dear husband took pride in who he had become and all that he had accomplished. He couldn't abide by the idea that someone might see him as anything but that. Embracing vulnerability allows us to open ourselves up to others for help. We pull back the curtain and enable them to see the demons we've been fighting or the infirmities that have assailed us. I was fortunate he only wanted to maintain that sense of pride with others. For him, it was somehow a source of his dignity. With me, he had let it go. I had always known that we trusted each other completely. It was in moments like this I knew that to be an absolute truth.

That following day after taking the girls to school and distracting myself with work, I checked in on him. As I spoke to him, there was a faraway look in his eye. It was a chilling look that told me he was struggling. He was struggling to recognize and make sense of his surroundings. He had retreated inward, and we were unable to connect like we usually did. I didn't know if he just didn't understand me or just didn't want to respond. Terror gave way to panic. I no longer knew what to do. I no longer knew how to make him comfortable. He was at a point where he depended on me entirely, and all I could think was that my next step would be to let him down. I couldn't do that and let him keep up this facade of pride. I couldn't go on alone. I took his hand and sat on the edge of the bed. I had always liked holding his hand. It seemed to always fit perfectly into my own. But this time, his grip was weak. I told him that I could no longer give him all the care he needed. I had to call his parents and ask them to come. His first impulse was to resist, but his ultimate reaction was a reluctant nod.

How do you make that phone call? The walk to my study was the stuff made from nightmares. It felt hard to move my legs. The floor was sticky, and it pulled my feet to it. The hallway got longer and longer with each step. What would I say? How would I open that conversation without completely breaking down? Like anything else, I overthought this. I overthought it a thousand times on the way to my study to get my phone. How would I tell two beautiful people that their baby boy was not well and that he hadn't wanted them to know? Would they blame me? Would they blame me further by thinking I hadn't been taking care of him? I dialed the number, and his father answered. I broke down completely.

They only lived two and a half hours away. They would be there as soon as they could. In the meantime, I knew I had to get Jayson to a wound care appointment. There was so much being done to try to get the scratch on his leg to heal. Healing is evidently tricky in the presence of edema.

I helped him get dressed in a pair of comfortable yet fashionable sweatpants. He had made a point earlier in his illness to ask that I keep several pairs of his best sweatpants clean. He slipped on his house shoes, and I got his portable oxygen concentrator. We began our trek across the house to the garage. He held on to me; his steps were slow and uncertain. I could feel his anguish with each step that he took. Not only was he in physical pain trying to walk, but it pained him to be dependent. I could tell with each step that there was a desire to do it on his own — to push me aside and to cry out that he could do it on his own. But he knew he couldn't. So he didn't say anything and just keep plodding forward. I never once got impatient or tried to push him too hard. I simply held on tight and steadied him. As we got to the garage, he stepped toward the driver's side of the car. He still wanted to drive. He still wanted to be independent and take care of himself. I quietly put my hand on his shoulder and whispered in his ear, "I can't let you do that. It just isn't safe." He quietly nodded, and I helped him into the passenger's side of the car.

The wound care facility was based at a hospital that was less than a mile from our house, but for some reason it felt like it was 25 miles away. His silence made the drive feel like it was longer than what it really was. He was reticent as we drove away. It felt as if in that time and space, everything was slowing down. The sun was out, and it was a warm winter's day. As he leaned back, his head tilted so that he could be fully in the sun. I could tell he loved the warmth. Ever since I had known him, he had easily gotten cold. On this day, the gentle warmth of the sun gave him a little kindness.

When we arrived at the hospital, despite having handicapped plates on the car, there were no empty spaces near the doors to park. I had to park away from the entrance and leave him in the car while I went in to find a wheelchair. You never really think of the little things that can make life easier for someone who's challenged until you're that someone. Fortunately, there was a herd of wheelchairs corralled just inside the entrance. I picked the cleanest one that was available.

The wound care office was on the first floor. So thankfully, we didn't have to navigate an elevator. When the receptionist welcomed us, she made it a point to raise her voice to make sure that Jayson could hear and understand her. It reminded me of how people tend to talk to the elderly struggling with hearing loss and dementia. I wanted to tell her that wasn't necessary — barely a year ago he was able to run two miles a couple of times a week for exercise. But, I knew he was already showing some signs of confusion. I put the thought aside.

However, while they changed his dressing, they continued to use the same tone of voice the whole time. I don't know why it bothered me so much but it did. I could tell they were concerned by his confusion. The appointment took longer than it usually did because they wanted to recommend special compression wear for him. I can't even remember exactly what it was because we never even made it to the appointment they had scheduled for us. The entire wound care appointment had made him tired. He needed to rest.

That evening, he sat on the hearth of the fireplace. I could tell his parents were shaken to see him that way. Like me, they had only known him as an incredible force. He was a stranger in his weakness. I had shared with them my struggle of trying to get him to the hospital and how he had resisted. His father followed me to the garage as I took a trash bag out to the bin. I knew he had wanted to say something in private. He had wanted to say something to me so as not to upset Jayson's mother or Jayson. He simply said, "It's time. You know what you need to do." And he was right. I knew that the care I could provide was no longer enough.

His condition was rapidly declining, and he needed medical expertise that I couldn't offer.

I sat down beside my husband and held his hand once again. I told him we had to go. This time he didn't resist. He simply nodded. I packed a bag for him, we kissed the girls and his parents and helped him to the car. The 30-minute drive to the hospital was long and painful. I tried not to let him see me cry. How could he feel secure if the one who was supposed to take care of him was breaking down? I guess I had a bit of my own pride about me. When we arrived, they asked him what the date was, and he got it wrong. With a searing pain in my heart, I knew this was the beginning of the end.

That had been five days earlier. And now, here we were. Between the doctors' advice and his wishes, all we could do was to make him comfortable. I wasn't even sure we'd been able to achieve that. The gray day gave way to a black, velvet night and a chill hung in the air. I was still curled up in the chair with my blanket wrapped around me. A tray of untouched food sat on the bed table. I held his hand and counted the increasing seconds between each breath. He brought me immense joy and healing in our life together, but at that moment, I felt inadequate for him. He had often called me his Superman, but I wasn't enough to save him. His breathing became more and more labored, and I held his hand more tightly. I loved him more than I had ever loved anyone, more than I thought I could ever love anyone. I didn't know whether to be thankful or terrified that I had been given the privilege of holding his hand as he slipped away. I had promised him "until death do us part." I was never one to break a promise. He took his last breath, and my heart shattered into a thousand irreparable pieces. How do you un-break a heart?

I said goodbye and kissed him as I stroked his hair. Then suddenly, I panicked, ran for the door, and stumbled into the young nurse coming into the room. I broke down and wept. All I could say is, "He's gone! He's gone! He's gone!" over and over until the words stuck in my throat, and I wanted them to be a lie. She nervously got her stethoscope and listened intently. I could tell that she was early in her career and this was not the experience she wanted. It was almost as if I could see her compose herself. She looked at me and nodded with an ethereal kindness and compassion. "I'll get my supervisor," she said as she turned and left the room. He came, he examined, and he concurred. "I'm so sorry for your loss." Was he? He had never met me. He had never met my husband. How could he know how sorry he needed to be? I had to breathe. Jayson often had told me that health care professionals have to balance compassion with difficult news. I was irrational. He had done what he needed to do and acknowledged my fresh pain the best he could.

I called my husband's father. I'd promised I would. Voicemail. I called his sister, and again, all I could say was, "He's gone" Then I called my mother. Do grown men still need their mothers? They do. "He's gone, mother. He's gone." I wept. At that moment, any gift for speech that I had ever had seemed to have vanished that night. I didn't want to believe that those were the only words I could say. Yet they kept coming, as did the tears. He was gone! Everything that made up his essence had vanished.

I found out later from the chaplain that I would need to have his body moved right away. There was no morgue at the hospital. Hadn't there been a morgue when I worked there? I couldn't remember. Again, there was a feeling of panic. This was such an important decision, and everyone had been telling me that I had time. I no longer had that time. I rummaged through the sitting area of his room. I was looking for the list that Hospice had left me of the funeral homes and crematoriums that were available. Hospice. I hadn't called them. I dialed. They said they would have someone out right away.

I stumbled through the list and frantically reviewed family funeral homes, bargain crematoriums, and those run by "corporate death." I settled on one that appeared to be something in between, and that random selection ended up being a perfect choice. Whether guided by fate or the recipient of dumb luck, I had managed to pick a funeral home filled with genuine compassion. The funeral director called me back promptly. Her voice was calm and reassuring. She made no assumptions, but asked if I'd like to hear about what they could offer. She reassured me that even if I chose not to use their services, they would make sure his body was taken care of until I had made my choice. In those few words, she completely removed a measure of panic. We settled on the services they would provide, and she assured me that her team would be there within a couple of hours and that I didn't need to worry. She recommended I go home and rest and that she would call me later in the day to finish up the details.

When the hospice worker arrived, she hugged me. She was so kind, but matter of fact. Her gray ponytail made her look both youthful and wise. She had an old Austin unpretentious demeanor. The nurse asked if it was okay if they prepared the body. What did that even mean? I said yes out of trust, and they proceeded ever so gently. They quickly and respectfully removed every monitor and the IV line. They reclined him flat and pulled the sheets up around him, and smoothed them ever so perfectly. They smoothed his hair so that he looked as handsome as he always had. The nurse and the social worker hugged me. Could they tell I was destroyed on the inside?

There is something about the immediate toll of grief that feels like surrender, especially if you've been sitting vigil. All you want to do is rest, but even that makes you feel guilty. They told me I didn't need to wait for the funeral home staff. They told me I had done all I needed to do. Had I? Surely there was more. I hadn't saved him. I wanted to exhaust every detail to be sure I had done everything I could for him. Then the words came back, "He's gone." They told me to take my time.

And take my time, I did. I gazed at his sweet and beautiful face. I traced every one of our 16 years together — the laughter, the tears, every moment that we took on the world together. Would I ever be that strong again? I ran my fingers through his hair, smoothing it even more so that the part was perfect. I told him again how much I loved him. I kissed his forehead, already cold to the touch, and then one last proper kiss. I left the room, walking backward. I looked at him as long as I could. This was it. These would be my last memories, and if I turned, they might be lost.

Had I done them right? Would I be able to recall them all and in enough detail? Was it enough to honor him? Was it enough? I slipped out the door and closed it ever so softly. I turned to walk to the elevator. Somewhere in the background, I heard the nurse say, "We'll watch over him until they come." I acknowledged her with a grateful nod. At least, I think I acknowledged her. I hope I hadn't been rude. I didn't know how to grieve like this. The tears started again as I began driving home, and they didn't stop. They haven't stopped.

2

How Do You Tell a Child?

We sat around on the couches in the gathering room in the early hours of the morning. The drive home from the hospital had been a blur. It was, fortunately, a route I had driven many times throughout my life. So I knew how to navigate it instinctually. I looked around the dimly lit room at my family; everyone was solemn and in shock. We knew this had been coming. We had been with him all week, watched the decline, held each other's hands, and looked the other way when we each had our moment of denial.

Now here we sat, with quiet tears and disbelief. I looked at my parents, who had loved and supported me through the 16 years of my relationship. I had watched them grow to love my husband as we spent time vacationing together and gathering for holidays. I could see their hearts breaking for me at that moment. I looked at my in-laws and the deep sadness on their faces. His parents had lost their baby boy, who had grown up to be such a spectacular man. His sister had lost her baby brother. They would all go on to grieve in their way, and I wondered then if they would be okay. Even in my grief, I was worried about everyone else.

Of course, I was most concerned about my daughters. In a cruel twist, they had been given a front-row seat to their Daddy's death.

They had watched his decline. But for now, they lay sleeping and unaware of the news that their remaining parent would soon deliver.

I had so many more decisions to make and had just made some of the most difficult of my life. His body was being cared for, so that gave me some comfort. Of course, I was going to have to plan his memorial service. Some friends still had to be told. I'd need to make a list. Lists have always comforted me and at least given me a false sense of control. But then the thought gripped me and terrified me; I would need to tell my daughters. They were sleeping, and I should let them sleep. I remember thinking at that moment that nothing would be worse than to be yanked out of slumber to be told one of your parents had died.

I remember announcing that decision to the room. Perhaps I was looking for validation; maybe I wanted to make the plan real. I can't remember if anyone even responded, although I'm pretty sure there were at least quiet nods. I'd tell my children when they woke up. The lump was already forming in my throat. Somewhere, deep down, very deep down, was a feeling of anger and quiet rage at this injustice. What had they done to deserve this? These two little girls, so wanted and so planned were still brimming with innocence. My instinct had always been to protect them, and I would have saved them from this if I could have. The weight of being the bearer of such news was suffocating.

I can't remember at what point I had decided that I would like to be a father. I had come out later in life, and nothing about that path had been easy. I was married, and the relationship with my wife became collateral damage to my finding the courage to speak my truth. It was another time of pain, of letting go, and of acceptance. But, it is another story entirely. Out I was. I was ready to be accepted by my people and be a part of something I felt like I belonged. Much to my chagrin, the gay community collectively yawned. My story was just another story of a broken man finding his way in a sea of lost and broken men. It was a time when our society had damaged so many of us. I had to look inward and find my self-reliance; my path was not about to get any easier.

After coming out, I often asked myself the question, "How does a single gay man create a family?" That was a question for which I had no answer. It was a question that scared me too. After all, I was in my 30s and still battling demons. So, I did what I do best. I researched. I read books on Russian adoptions, Chinese adoptions, Central American adoptions, and South American adoptions. The conclusion was always the same. It would be next to impossible for me partly because I was a single gay man and partly because the expense was staggering. Even the success stories were full of struggle, and I saw so many happy men working to raise their baby under the mountain of debt it had taken to create their family. So the books lined my bookshelf; they were my dream deferred. They became a symbol of quiet hope that faded with every passing day.

When Jayson and I started dating, I remember one of the first times he was at my apartment. As anyone would do, he was looking around and taking in my space. As apartments went, it was a nice one, laid out like a small house. The living room had a built-in bookcase. While I was making drinks in the kitchen just around the corner, he began commenting on the books he could see. When he came to the books on adoption, there was a decided change in his voice. He exclaimed with great excitement that he had thought about the same thing! As we sat on my futon, having drinks and getting to know each other, we lamented the same barriers. Both dreams remained deferred.

As our lives progressed, houses were bought, sold, and built. Not much else, if anything, had been said about the situation. We had gone on about building a life together. We had fallen into routines broken up by the adventure of travel. Somewhere, post-adventure and settled into the comfort of familiarity, the conversation happened. We were sitting on the back patio of the first house we had lived in together. We had enjoyed an evening with friends and talked about the evening and life itself as we sat outside.

We tended to do that quite a bit; talk about life. There was this strange power we had together. We'd come up with grand ideas and then pool our talents to make them happen. There was this combination of determination, planning, and execution that had created a wonderful life for us. But it was in that moment, talking outback, that we realized something was missing.

"We should start a family!" I'm not sure who said it first. But the words hung on the night air like a challenge, like a plan, like hope. We just looked at each other for a long while, smiling. "Are we serious?" he asked. I remember that feeling like it was yesterday. There was a sudden lightness to that hope of creating a family with this man. Our lives were brimming over with love; why wouldn't we share that? But how? The how was always my queue to research, to propose a plan, to educate us. Would we adopt? Would we pursue open adoption? Would we foster to adopt? Would we pursue surrogacy? Each of these was a viable option, but there would be a financial cost and an emotional cost for each option. We needed to fully understand each approach and what going down that path would mean. I had my task cut out for me. We held each other tightly that night. A buzz of excitement burst into our lives in just a mere moment. But, as I have learned repeatedly, mere moments can change your life forever.

It took months of research. But why wouldn't it? A decision to start a family was not a decision to be entered into lightly. It would change everything about the life we knew, not to mention the obligation we'd have to a child who'd be depending on us for everything. We wanted to do it right, and not just right, but suitable for us and right for the child we'd be parenting. After a great deal of exploring, debate, and thought, we decided to pursue the path of surrogacy. The longer-term plan was to have two children, but for now, the focus was just getting started. I found an agency that would work with gay men. Little did I know how fortunate it was to find that agency at the time or what they would come to mean to us. At least at that time, the world of surrogacy was a complicated mix of legal agreements, high emotions, and trust. We would find each one of those violated at some point, and I'm not sure we could have navigated that without the support of the agency we selected.

I'll never forget when our oldest daughter arrived. It had been a typical day around the house for me. Jayson had gone off to work for a 24-hour shift at 7:00 that morning. It was a Wednesday. I had done some consulting and coaching work during the day while temperatures outside dropped. The ground was white with a mix of ice and snow. It was the kind of weather we tend to get in February in Texas as winter finally takes hold just in time to let go. I had curled up on the couch in our bedroom and started the gas fireplace. It was time to unwind and watch some TV and text with Jayson as his schedule allowed. We always had an ongoing text thread. It allowed us to keep a conversation going even when there were significant gaps because we were busy with work. We always felt connected.

Then the message came through. "Pack a bag. We need to leave." What? I couldn't imagine what was going on. The subsequent texts made it clear. Our baby was coming early. Our surrogate was on her way to the hospital. Fortunately, I had a bag packed for the baby — all the things she'd need after she arrived. I'm a planner, and I had planned everything down to the car seat. I quickly packed duffle bags for Jayson and me as I waited for him to get home. I left his bag open so he could check it — something I always did for him. He never seemed to be missing anything because I had thought of it all, but it seemed to reassure him, and I didn't mind. It had just become part of how we worked together. One of the neonatologists came in to cover the shift for Jayson. All I could think about was how we had probably ruined his night. There would need to be profuse thank yous. I would come to know him better over time and learn that kindness was just his thing.

We had to make it to Fort Worth that night with ice-covered roads and snow on the ground. We were quickly going through checklists and reminders for each other because we didn't have much time.

Our birth plan and surrogate contract called for a cesarean section. Jayson kept reminding me that we might not make it before the procedure was complete. Caring for newborns was, after all, his field. He had attended more cesarean section procedures than he could count. I remember going over and over in my mind about how fast we could safely go on what is usually a problematic interstate highway, even in the best of conditions. Little did I know at that moment that we had far more time than I realized.

Our surrogate hijacked the birth. We discovered later that she had never intended to go through with the C-section. In all of our early discussions, we had been very clear that if she chose to do a vaginal birth after her previous C-sections, we just weren't going to be a match. Jayson knew all too well the potential of adverse outcomes surrounding vaginal births after a cesarean, and it just produced too much fear and anxiety. We offered our support for her and wished her the best in finding just the right couple with whom to work. She came back to us, and she offered to deliver via C-section. It was all a lie.

With every contraction, our baby's heart rate decelerated. Something wasn't right. We kept pleading for help. We were stuck with a contractual agreement that was meaningless at that moment. The nurses shut us out and classified us as the enemy. The relations deteriorated, and the next 24 hours were some of the most anxiety-ridden of my life. None of this was going to plan.

Of all the things that stick with me from staying in the hospital, trying to rest and waiting on labor to progress is one of the most vivid. We were powerless to do anything and had to spend our remaining time in the hospital's large waiting room. You could see the snow outside. It was still cold, and because one entire wall of the waiting room was glass, the cold crept in and made itself at home. I sat in a sea of green, vinyl couches and chairs that stretched out across the football-sized waiting room. My parents had arrived. I could tell my mother was doing her best to help manage what should be a joyful time, but that had turned fearful.

I remember sitting up after having laid on one of the horrible vinyl couches, peeling my cheek off the cushion, to see Jayson talking to my mother near the vending machines. I saw him break down and cry, something I had rarely seen in our life together, and my mother hugged him. She is a counselor by training and just a highly empathetic person in general. I could tell by that exchange just how scared my husband was and I sat there choking on my fear.

Almost 24 hours, a nuchal cord, and shoulder dystocia later, I held our baby girl. It is hard to describe what you feel as a new parent when you first hold your baby. There are so many emotions and an overwhelming sense of wonder. But the thing I felt the most was protective. She was so tiny and defenseless and utterly dependent on her parents to be her advocate and take care of her. What followed was a hospital ordeal that I wouldn't wish on anyone.

We were stuck with a pediatrician and a group of nurses who didn't think a baby girl should go home with two men. The bigotry was palpable. They treated us with so much disregard and disrespect. While they tried to hold the baby as long as they could while claiming she wasn't eating correctly, we knew better. Her feeding chart was exemplary even to me as someone with no experience, but especially to my husband who had extensive expertise in the field. When they finally discharged us, I have never been so happy to leave a place in my life. Sadly, it was only the beginning of my experience with people who think gay men shouldn't be parents.

We moved heaven and earth to bring our first child into the world. We'd do that again for our second child but in a much less hostile environment. There were lessons learned by us all, including our agency, with the first surrogacy journey. With those lessons in mind, we matched with our second surrogate and began our journey again when our eldest was two. As fate would have it, we were fortunate, and the match was much, much better.

The relationship felt right from the beginning, and the experience when our youngest arrived was so much different. There was a camaraderie in the hospital as our sweet little girl bounced back and forth between the loving couple who brought her into the world and her two daddies who would bring her home. That connection has lasted until this day.

While my life as a single parent is busy and chaotic, and the life of our surrogate is just as busy with her own family, we manage to stay connected on social media. I send pictures as I can, and she gets to see the life moments I post. The one thing that still stands out to me about the woman who brought my second child into the world is just how big her heart is. She showed us so much kindness, love, and grace, and I have learned that's just how she lives. She made up for so much of the pain I lived through during my first journey. I am forever grateful to her.

Those thoughts rumbled around my head the entire night I tried to sleep. Those two little girls sleeping upstairs were so wanted and so loved — and it took a monumental effort to get them here. Even after their arrival, there were so many hoops to jump through to build our family. So many times, we had to prove that our girls had a biological connection to us. So many times, we had to produce court documents to prove we were a family. Even after laws were changed and both of our names were on their birth certificates, that still wasn't enough. We constantly had to battle the fact that so many people still didn't think two men should raise children, especially little girls.

Those thoughts always surface one of the most challenging encounters I had. We had gone out to do some after Christmas shopping. If there was one thing my husband truly loved, it was a deal. And, of course, the markdowns on the day after Christmas can be irresistible. He had taken our youngest and had gone to browse while I took the oldest to the restroom. She would soon turn 3. When we came out of the bathroom, she innocently asked where her Daddy was. So we played a game. She would call, "Daddy, Daddy, come out, come out wherever you are." As we played and laughed, a woman approached us and spoke directly to my child.

"Are you okay, little girl?" She asked indignantly.

"Please, don't speak directly to my daughter. How can I help you?" I said, coldly.

"Why is this little girl looking for her Daddy?"

"We're a two-dad family; my husband has our other daughter." I said, trying to hold my temper.

"I'll need to see them. I need to make sure you're not kidnapping this girl," she said with an air of superiority.

"No. Please stop harassing us and step away."

"I'm going to call security," she said threateningly.

"Please do — I'd like to have you removed for harassment."

I walked away with my daughter. As we made our way to the back of the store where the sale sections were, she popped out from an aisle and accosted us again by saying, "I'm going to call security."

I had had enough! In my most firm and theatrically trained voice, I called out, "Security! Security! A woman is trying to take my daughter!" She was shocked and took two steps back. She finally turned and walked away. I held my daughter close to me. Again, like they had so many times before, the feelings of protection were overwhelming. So many people felt like she didn't belong to me, and this day was proof that they would even try to take her away. Suddenly, standing in the bright, wide aisle of a big box store, I felt incredibly vulnerable. I had to protect my girls from those who would seek to do them harm. I had to protect them from all of those who believe that we shouldn't be a family.

But what kind of family were we now? How would I even begin to tell them, define for them, and help them see that even just the three of us would continue to be a family? How would they remember him? His decline was swift the last week of his life. He had very few lucid moments. I was fortunate enough to have brought our girls to see him when he first got moved to a hospice room in the hospital. He was alert and lucid. They both got to talk to him, kiss him, and most importantly tell him they loved him and hear him say it back. I think part of me knew, but I didn't want to admit to myself that this would be the last time they would ever see him.

The last words he said to them were, "I love you." I don't think there was ever a point after that when he would have been coherent enough to talk to them. I hope I did that right — I hope I gave them an excellent last moment to remember. We didn't know enough at the time that it was also goodbye. I still remember the last "I love you" I heard from him that week. In the end, I was the only one to utter the word goodbye.

Coffee. It's my morning go-to routine. On this particular morning, I needed it more than usual. I had slept fitfully, knowing what I had to do. The burden of it sat on my chest and made it hard to breathe. I knew they'd but up soon. We had a house full of family, and they would want to see them all. Every feeling of protection I have ever felt for either of them welled up inside me. I wanted to protect them from this! I wanted to spare them the heartache. I wanted to spare them having to work through such complicated feelings at such a young age. In their innocence, they didn't deserve this at all. But do any of us? There is a nasty side to life, and perhaps that's just part of the balance. My heart stopped cold when I heard their little feet on the stairs.

When they first wake up, there is something about children, their sleepy eyes, and their tousled hair all giving way to the energy and desire to play for the day. My two are no different. Piles of blonde hair were everywhere as they came down to see their family. The mood in the room was somber. The loss was only beginning to take hold, and we were taking the first step of our journey into the grief valley — an action that would be different for us all. None of us ever really grieve alike. Grief, I have found, is the mirror image to love, and we suffer according to how we loved. We all loved him differently.

My two little ones came to me and hugged me. They could sense something was not quite right. It was quiet. People were just sitting around the great room staring off into space. There was no laughter. Before there were questions and before anyone had to say or relive something they didn't want to, I pulled my girls into my bedroom and closed the door. The room had a soft and quiet glow to it, with the shades still down. I hadn't turned on any of the lights. We sat on the floor, and I held their hands. I could feel the lump forming in my throat and the telltale burning behind my eyes. I had to keep it together to at least be able to tell them. It was okay for me to cry in front of them, but I had to explain what happened first and do it clearly. After I delivered the news, they needed to know it was okay to cry as they figured out how to start to mourn.

I'll never forget the words. I chose them carefully, and they were the most difficult words I've ever had to speak in my life. "Girls, you remember how sick Daddy was when you went to visit last time?"

They nodded. Two sets of wide eyes, one clear blue, and the other a deep brown, looked at me expectantly. It made what I was saying even more difficult. "Things continued to get worse. He fought it the best he could, but it wasn't enough. Last night, while I was with him, it all got too much, and he died."

"What do you mean he died?" my oldest asked. How should I answer that? It was an innocent enough question. She was trying to grasp the magnitude and meaning of what I was telling her. How could I blame her for not wanting to believe it initially? Did I really believe it? I tried to explain to them slowly and gently what had transpired.

"The illness got to be too much for his body. He's gone, girls. It's just us now."

"We'll never see him again?" she pressed.

"No, honey. We won't. We'll have to keep the memories Daddy left us."

Her eyes welled up with tears. The little one looked at her as if searching for a queue for her behavior. We were, indeed, in uncharted territory. This loss was their first experience with grief, and I had never lost a spouse. He was our source for so much laughter, joy and a sense of adventure. I tried my best to keep our conversation straightforward. "Everyone is sad today because we all miss him so much. So you'll see some of us cry today because we miss him. You might cry some today as well. That's okay. That's what happens when you lose someone you love. If you need to talk about it or talk about what you remember about him, you go right ahead. It's how we keep him alive in our hearts."

I cried. I couldn't hold it back any longer. My heart ripped from my chest, and pain then filled the void. I pulled my girls close to me as they began to weep. I took a deep breath. I inhaled and exhaled to help me through my emotions and their emotions. I will never forget. They smelled so much of little girl things. The cotton candy and sugar plum shampoo filled my nose. The fragrance was a reminder of how little they were. A reminder of their childhood innocence — unspoiled, untouched by the cruel realities of life. I held on even tighter as they began to weep too. All I could think about was whether or not I'd be enough for them. In just a matter of seconds, my mind raced through being able to provide for them financially, emotionally, and would I be enough to help them become the adults they needed to become.

How the mind can fit so much into such a small amount of time, I'll never know. But one of the oddest thoughts that hit me was a memory of something Jayson had said when moving into this house. "We have the perfect prom staircase!" Prom. I paused for a moment and realized that I'd be the only one to take their pictures and to see them off on their special evening. The fact that he'd miss that made me incredibly sad. It's only one moment of many that won't include him going forward. Would I be enough?

How do you tell a child they've lost their parent? I'm not sure I have an answer. As I discovered, you just have to say it to them and

28

let them know that you hurt as well. At least that was my approach. It set the stage for us to talk about it any time they need to. We still talk about it. It crops up when I least expect it to. I think it's still especially hard for my youngest. We talk often of things that their Daddy would do. I revisit memories and stories for them over and over. I want the canon of those stories to be well remembered and often told. As I write this, we are almost three years away from that fateful morning conversation.

I still get a little girl coming to me and telling me she's sad. She'll curl up in my lap or next to me in bed. There is a bit of fear there. She fears losing her memories of him. She was so young when he died that she may not be able to remember as much as she would like. There is a certain saving grace to all of this technology we deal with. I have pictures for her. I have videos of him holding her and singing to her. I have preserved every memory that I can, and I'll soon put them all together for her. They both still look to me for clues on how to navigate all of this. Just like the morning I told them, I have no good answers for them. They have to find their own path, and that is a terribly difficult thing to watch as a parent. But, I can hold their hand when they need it, remind them that they're always loved, and do my best to create a life for them.

3

The Painfully Long Ending

Some say that losing a loved one, especially a spouse, is physiologically traumatic, much like being severely wounded. Shock is the physical reaction that we can experience to a traumatic event. The immediate aftermath of the death of a loved one is complicated, and the deep wound of the loss can create shock and what I have come to call grief aftershocks. For me, grief aftershocks are the waves of physical reactions that continue to come over and over in those first few weeks after a loss. Loss is different for everyone, but losing a spouse can be significant and create a depth of trauma we have not yet known, and the shock that accompanies it can be just as substantial. These complicated and powerful feelings get wrapped up in the blanket term of grief. Everyone likes to think they know how to define grief for you because, for many, grief has a proper definition, and they'll expect you to follow that definition. What they don't realize is that there is no proper grief.

We all grieve differently. Grieving requires us to have an awareness of our emotions and their underlying causes. Self-awareness is no easy task, even in the best of times, so it is a tough challenge when you find yourself in the depth of sorrow. Others like to tell you how to understand your feelings by constantly outlining the stages of grief for you. They think the stages of grief are linear, and you

31

experience them one at a time on your way to healing, or as many like to put it — on your way to "moving on" or "moving forward."

I don't think Elisabeth Kübler-Ross, a Swiss-American psychiatrist, had a linear progression in mind when she published *On Death and Dying*, where she discussed her theory of the first five stages of grief. Actually, a linear progression is more straightforward as a guidepost to those who want us to simply "get over it." The truth is one can experience these stages in any order and, at times, all at once. At least that has been my experience. Ultimately, there is no empirical evidence to support the Kübler-Ross model. So it is certainly not a one-size-fits-all approach to grief. One of the worst questions I experienced in the time after my husband's death was, "What stage are you in?"

I hated the question. It felt too cold and too clinical for people with no experience in psychology to even ask. It felt like a random and heartless question. The underlining tone made me feel as if throughout my grieving I was supposed to follow some sort of clinical pattern entirely devoid of the possibility of anyone ever experiencing their own grief on their own time and in their own way without following any specific model. Did they think I was simply going through a checklist? In some ways, I also felt offended because each time I heard that question I felt that my feelings were being discarded and labeled based on others perception of what the five stages of grief should look like, what they should feel like, when they should happen, how they should happen and the order they should follow. Why should I have to box my feelings up into some neatly categorized container with specific labels? Doing that would have made them feel better and helped their understanding. But this wasn't about them. This journey was about my own grief.

I had some time to prepare myself emotionally, though his decline accelerated in the end much to my surprise and dismay. My husband's symptoms came on suddenly. We had returned from a fabulous vacation with family, and it was as if his body was coming unraveled. I would immediately research every sign to understand it, and understand if we could beat it. That process became harder and harder. In my mind, I would rail against it all as things progressed and the prognosis became direr and direr.

Ultimately, I had made my peace with the fact that we probably had between five and ten years. However, I was still angry. I wanted him to be around to see his daughters graduate from high school. I wanted to hold his hand on the beach in Cancun many more times. I wanted to plan life. It was one of the most exciting things we did together. We created plans and made them happen. That process was one of the greatest joys I had in life. But now, those plans took a different turn and weren't easy to discuss. But I'm glad we did have those discussions because ten years turned to five, and five years turned to five days. The trauma of his loss was real and visceral. That loss ripped away a part of me. The shock left me breathless.

As anyone familiar with post-traumatic stress disorder will tell you, feeling afraid is a common symptom. Fear is a powerful emotion that can grip you and put you directly in the throes of panic. This was an academic fact that I knew but not a real one I had experienced. The experience of it was overwhelming. Within a single moment, I looked out across the plan we had laid out for our lives, and realized he would not be there to make that plan happen with me. I felt horror in thinking I had to do it myself and that my daughters would be counting on me for every single piece of it. Breathing became difficult because, in the span of a single moment, I lost confidence in myself, felt a huge desire to be protective of my children, and was immediately trying to make adjustments to the plan so it would require less from me. The questions that flooded my mind kept coming one right after the other.

How would I make a living? After all, I was between jobs at the time, and would the new job be the right choice? (It ultimately wasn't.) Would I have the ability to make enough money to make up for the lack of Jayson's income? Would I be able to give my children everything that they needed from me, both financially and emotionally? With every single question came more and more self-doubt. It was emotionally crushing.

In the days that followed losing him, I had to plan so many things. It was almost overwhelming. I met with my in-laws at the funeral home to discuss how the memorial service should look. I'll never forget sitting in the big, comfortable chair at a dark wooden conference table in a wood-paneled room. The thick carpeting made the room extra quiet. The staff was so incredibly professional — a fact that I later realized went a long way to making all of us feel more at ease.

First came the paperwork. I never realized just how much paperwork was involved when someone dies. Jayson had chosen cremation. This set the stage for the first order of business. There were questions and proof to confirm that the funeral home did indeed have the right body. I then had to give my permission for cremation.

But then they asked one of his parents to sign as next of kin. While we had been legally married for almost ten years, Texas had only recently recognized our marriage. There was a part of me that felt deeply offended because I wasn't acknowledged as his next of kin on paper, but the other part of me also recognized the practical nature of it all. With all his immediate family gathered in one room, it made sense to be sure that no one had a question about his last wishes. The entire process was such a blur.

In the end, his mother signed — she certainly wasn't going to go against his wishes. Perhaps things might have been different for another family. My family was connected. Our primary goal was to follow Jayson's last wishes, and his family saw me as his widower regardless of what anyone else might have thought at that time. It's a love I still enjoy to this day.

That was only the beginning. There were so many decisions to be made. All I could think about was how practical Jayson would have wanted me to be. He was never one to waste money, and we jointly talked about all of our spending decisions. Yet, here I was with only myself to lean on. The decisions were all mine. I had the luxury of having some input from family, but ultimately I was the one to decide.

The first decision I had to make was for a cremation tray. I had no idea such a thing existed. The very idea of it seemed awkward. In the movies, cremation always seemed to happen on some metal tray, but suddenly I found myself presented with options ranging from the economical cardboard tray to options made of wood and lined with silk. After all, we were talking about something to be burned with his body. I couldn't bring myself to buy the more expensive models. I had to trust my gut on this one. But what swayed my decision in the end? A pillow. For some reason, I wanted him to have a pillow to rest his head as we carried out his final wishes. My choice was both economical and environmentally friendly. Those features would have both scored points with him.

Points. I was still keeping score as if any of this mattered to him. I had to remind myself that what mattered was that I carried out his last wishes just as he wanted, and I had to be honest that some of the choices were entirely for me.

Flowers. I hadn't thought I'd need them since we were doing cremation, but then I realized there would need to be a memorial service. His friends would want to say goodbye to the man they'd known for so long. I wanted to be able to give them that closure. There would need to be flowers near the urn. It was so odd to call what I had chosen an urn. It was a box. It was a beautiful, inlaid wooden box. We had both decided that we wanted our ashes scattered and not to end up on a mantle top as a knick-knack. I chose the box so that our daughters could use it to store mementos later.

I couldn't even think about the pilgrimage we'd need to make to scatter the ashes. My daughters would require years of growing before appreciating the trip and understanding what we were doing. I had to make my peace because we had discussed that, and I knew I had time. There was no hurry. But the flower decision stayed immediate. There was photo after photo of beautiful flowers from which I could choose. What would he like best? When had I seen him like a particular flower? Could I even remember in this state? It turns out I could.

There was a 50-year-old oak tree in the back yard in the first house we shared despite the house being a new build. There were so many memories of us making that house a home together. One of the projects we did was the backyard. We enhanced the drainage with a winding, dry creek bed, and a raised patio with herringbone pavers. There was a certain satisfaction knowing that we had built it ourselves. I'm not sure I would have ever attempted something so ambitious, but he could always inspire me. Jayson was fearless when it came to those things. It was because of him we decided to lay tile in the house ourselves. Of course, we didn't just lay tile, but we laid chiseled edge travertine tile in a Versailles pattern. It was so beautiful, and I was continually in wonder at the fact that we had done that. That same wonder carried to the backyard, and all the beauty that seemed to unfold under the sprawling branches of that oak tree.

To complete the look, Jayson wanted a white garden in the back corner of the yard. There was a pie-shaped bed there, and it wasn't long before it was blooming with beautiful white flowers. Against a backdrop of white, heirloom roses were a line of beautiful calla lilies. He loved them and thought they were beautiful. I'm not sure if I smiled when that memory hit me, but it washed over me, and I remembered sitting outside and admiring those flowers with him.

As I watched the flower choices scroll on the screen in front of me in that conference room of the funeral home, there it was, a simple yet incredibly full vase of calla lilies. That's what I chose. There was a certain peace I had about that decision. While I'm sure he would have liked it, moreover I liked it as well. It reminded me of one of the many, many intimate conversations we had as we spent time together. There was nothing better for me than spending time with him, and those flowers punctuated that idea for me. They would be perfect.

From that point, I'd need to choose music and a passage for the program. Fortunately, there was time to think through those. I took a look at some of the suggested selections thinking I might find something that would work. Nothing. None of them seemed to fit. They either seemed too trite, too sappy, or just inappropriate for him. I needed something to capture his essence and how I wanted to remember him, and how others would remember him. Choosing the music had the same challenge. He loved music and was constantly singing. His voice could fill the house. I needed to think through all of the favorite songs he'd ever mentioned to me. I needed to review his playlists for clues to find the perfect few melodies that would forever be tied to him and that would forever remind me of him whenever I heard them. I wasn't fully aware at the time just how that decision would irrevocably change songs I loved.

Later that afternoon, the only feeling I could muster was numbness. Did I have to do all of this? Was this happening to me? It was all so hard to believe. Nothing could have prepared me for what I was going through despite any talk, planning, or even any imagining. The shock of what I was experiencing continued. And that's the curious part of grief, isn't it? We are traumatized by the immediate loss, but that trauma continues and is unintentionally exacerbated by all of the things that society expects of us. All I wanted to do was to be alone with my pain — to get to know it, understand it, and name it. I was afforded no such luxury, just as I would expect thousands of those grieving experience. Life often won't allow it. I had two little girls who were depending on me. I had family who needed me to be strong. Stolen moments crying on the floor of my closet would be about all I'd get. I remember the panic I felt after letting go. There, on the floor, surrounded by his clothes, terror would grip me because I had to keep it together. So many things needed to be done; there were so many expectations to be met.

Being a planner is in my nature. Perhaps it is a control method — if I can plan for it, I can control it. Any time that we'd travel, I'd plan everything in great detail. I'll never forget how much we used to laugh about it; it was the year we would refer to as our year of travel. One of our trips was a trip with my parents to England and France. We only had seven days and I wanted to maximize every minute of it. I created a full itinerary, planned for everything, and booked particular tours intended to give us the most for our time. After all, my husband and my parents had never been, and I wanted their experience to be a good one. From touring the haunts of Jack the Ripper in London to toasting champagne atop the Eiffel Tower, we got to experience so many beautiful things together. But sometimes, it's the unplanned and the unexpected that can deliver joy too. My parents had opted out of the Eiffel Tower tour, citing crowds, wait times, and claustrophobia. One of the underlying tenants of travel in our family is to follow your bliss. You don't have to do anything you don't want to, and you're free to find things that make you happy. So they went back to the flat for a relaxing pizza night.

We chose to stand in the queue, and stand in the queue we did! The elevator up to the second level was packed. We were shoulder to shoulder with as many people as they could fit in that tiny space. My parents had made the right choice for them. We had to laugh, as the crowds were not unexpected. As we spent time hanging out and enjoying the views while waiting on our turn to go to the top, we heard a young Scottish man who was vacationing with his parents and siblings exclaim, "What will you remember about your time in Paris? Standing in bloody queue!" We laughed so hard. Something about his anger, coupled with a beautiful accent, made his comment incredibly funny. Even now as I write about that memory, I can manage a smile. There was nothing quite like laughing with my husband; the laughs were belly laughs.

As the evening began to envelop Paris, we made it to the top of the tower. The vistas were breathtaking. We walked around the deck surrounded by the city's most beautiful landmarks — from the

Sacré-Coeur to the Louvre. The winding reflection of the Seine was a silver ribbon through one of the most beautiful cities in the world. We were both quiet for a time, being overtaken by the enormity of that moment. Whichever direction we looked, our eyes indulged in the beauty and history all around us. Then, as we looked behind us we realized we were right in front of the window where we could order champagne. So we did! Toasting each other with the city behind us, a smiling fellow tourist took our picture. It's a picture I treasure and a picture our children have grown to love as well. Our oldest daughter has asked me, more than once, if I will take her there so we can have our picture taken just like that. She'd even allow the little one to join. Despite being overwhelmed with the idea of getting back to Paris, my answer is always yes.

Once we descended from the top of the tower, night began to fall and the first hour of darkness was upon us. The tower illuminated as if with lightning, and the sparkles began. The sight was breathtaking from inside the lift. As we exited the tower, we walked to the center, looked up, and held hands. We looked at each other and smiled. This was our life together, and it was beautiful. While we walked back to our flat, there was a low and unexpected rumble in the sky. We continued our walk down ancient and winding streets, taking in the beauty of the architecture fashioned long before either of us had come to be. Suddenly, it began to rain. At first, it slowly caressed the city, and we wondered if we'd make it back before it got heavier. Yet, in a matter of moments, the mist of rain got thicker. Soon it turned into a real summer downpour. We ran and saw an alcove with an awning and quickly took cover in that small space.

I held him close, and we took a moment to kiss each other with giddy smiles. There we were, summertime in Paris, the streets drenched in the rain, and ducking under an awning for a romantic moment suspended in time. It was like a movie. As quickly as it had begun, the rain stopped, and we continued on our way. I had not really planned the timing of our visit to the tower with the lighting, nor had I planned that specific path back to the flat or the rain, but that unexpected part of the evening was one of the best experiences of my life. I'll never, ever forget the feeling of joy that I had as I fell asleep that night. Fast forward to today, joy has grown more difficult to find in my life. So the contrast to that moment is stark. It's my joy yardstick against which I measure so many of my experiences. It's a joy I hope to recapture — a joy I'll never forget.

As I continued to plan the memorial service in my mind, I found myself lost in reverie with moment after moment of our life together. No matter what I could come up with for the service, it was a flat coda on a beautiful and adventurous life. While I remembered the joy of so many beautiful moments together, I felt an overwhelming sadness as I had to go through those steps. I have heard people often talk about how grief and despair come in waves. Nothing for me was a wave at that time, but it was a perpetual drowning. I viewed everything from the bottom of a sea of mourning, and I kept reaching for something to save me — for something to keep me afloat— but everything I had worked so hard to build kept steadily slipping away. To some extent, it still does. The letting go is painfully long.

What is it about pictures that can be so powerful? Their ubiquity surrounds us in this modern life. We have pictures of so many moments of our lives. Well-curated pictures of dinners, which somehow seem to punctuate American excess, fill social media. There was something about planning a video montage as a mourning widower that felt commercial and oddly inappropriate. In the end, it was an opportunity to present the memories of my husband that would allow family and friends to both relive moments with him. I'm not sure how I would have felt seeing so many more pictures of his life before me. As I sat with his mother and sister and looked through the physical images from his life before me, I found myself falling for him all over again.

It was evident he had always had a zest for life. While we had logged hours and hours of deep conversation about our pasts, it was quite an experience to see it captured in photos. There were so many pictures of him smiling, laughing, and even being a little mischievous. We had both often said that we met each other at just the right time; a part of me felt a little cheated for not having known him earlier. I felt like I had missed out on so much, but then again, that could have just been me feeling like I had been cheated out of the life I had created with him. I was yearning for more time anywhere on the timeline. As I flipped from picture to picture, I found myself missing him more and more. I wasn't sure that was even possible. I would have given anything at that moment for one more smile, one more laugh, or even hearing how he used to say my name when he was exasperated with me. We all stopped talking as we looked at pictures; they transported each of us to our private place of loss. The warm silence of our own loss, of our memories, pierced our hearts. We gazed at each photo and absorbed every detail as time stood still flooding our hearts with tender memories. At that moment, nothing else mattered.

Planning a memorial service is supposed to be about honoring and celebrating the life of someone special. All of the work put into that kind of service holds a unique pain for the grieving. Every choice I had to make, from the flowers, to the music, to the pictures, made me relive almost every moment of my life with him. It created an underscore of everything I had built with him and then everything I had lost. In a way, it packaged up so much of what I had to let go. I'd never let him go, but so much of the life I had created with him was over. I had made so many plans that included him, plans that no longer made any sense without him in them. There was a master plan for our lives together with our children, and it was such a good one. So much of the foundation had been completed, and we were standing tall and happy on it as we looked at how we'd go forward. There was so much joy ahead of us and so many moments yet to be experienced as a couple, parents, and individuals. Planning his service reminded me that all of that is gone.

Once everything was planned, I tried to take a minute to have a sense of accomplishment, knowing that I had survived reliving all of those moments and making all of those decisions, but it was short-lived. Panic set in as I realized I still needed to plan a reception at the house for close family and friends after the service. I was no stranger to planning social events, but did I have to prepare one for the death of my husband? After a deep breath, I accepted that I did. Of course, I was not alone. My family and those I choose to call family all pitched in to help. My sister-in-law picked up the perfect plates and cutlery, my mother and mother-in-law helped me choose the food, and one of Jayson's dearest friends, whom I've since inherited as my own, picked it up. It would be casual. It would be fine. It would be enough.

My dark suit. Did it still fit okay? I had lost so much weight the week I spent with him in the hospital. Had the rebound started? If there was one thing my life taught me, I would eat my feelings. I had been so busy planning, organizing, and being numb that I had not taken the time to make sure the suit I would wear would fit or to even think about which tie would I choose? There were still so many decisions to be completed, and these were all for me. I had taken the time to select dresses for our girls to wear. They would be in classic black and white. It hurt to dress our children for his death. When I looked at myself in the mirror, it was surreal. The suit fit, but I was surprised by the look of sadness on my face. I'm not sure I'd ever seen myself look that sad. I had to look away and hope that I looked well enough for the service. Today would make things final, at least some things.

I paused before walking into the chapel and took a long deep breath. I needed to hold it together. There were already so many people gathering. I knew he was well-loved, but I'm not sure I expected the forming crowd — another deep breath. Most of my young life was about performing on stage. I knew how to control my emotions; I learned how to manage when all eyes were on me. As I took that first step down the aisle and looked up, I saw the flowers and the wooden urn on the table. His picture, one of the last I had taken of him during a happy time, sat beside the urn. I was not prepared for what I felt. I had never had to manage any emotion like that. I was suddenly out of my league. It felt as if the floor had been pulled out from under me, and I was falling with no end in sight. I felt an unsettling combination of terror, sadness, grief, and loneliness, all in a single moment of exquisite pain. Was it, or is it, even possible to feel this much pain? Could a human survive what had suddenly coalesced around me?

As I sat in the pew, I pulled my daughters close to me and wept. It was a weeping that comes from deep inside and breaks through any pretense or sense of control that we think we might have. I think people may have tried to say hello as they walked into the service, but my eyes were too blurred with tears to see who had said anything or even touched my shoulder. I kept trying to breathe. The only thing I could do was to disconnect from this feeling that was driving such a physical response from me. There was a full memorial service that had to take place. I didn't want to be there. All I could think was that it wasn't right. It shouldn't be happening. But it was…

The priest read from the *Book of Common Prayer*. All of the choices I had made for that portion quickly marched before me. I had spent so much time laboring over them that it felt anti-climactic. But I guess that was the point. The service proceeded smoothly, just as it was intended. When the priest yielded to Jayson's friends, who had prepared small eulogies for him, it was hard to hold back the tears again. These were people who had worked with him, gone to school with him, people who had shared experiences with him that had galvanized their friendship. I knew exactly what they had loved about him. So much of what he shared with his friends of himself was part of the bedrock of our relationship. At the core of our love and passion was a deep and abiding friendship infused with trust and vulnerability. I was reminded yet again of what I had lost, and it hurt.

As the service ended, the priest left so quickly I wasn't able to give him the honorarium I had worked so hard to remember to bring. I was then surprised by the people lining up to provide me with their condolences. Of course, there were so many of Jayson's friends and co-workers, but I think I was most surprised to see so many of my own. Some people only knew of Jayson through our conversations, but yet here they were. They came not only to pay their respects to Jayson but to support me as well. That made a huge and unanticipated impact on me. It changed how I see some of my friends and colleagues. Not that I had looked at them negatively, but I now see them with a deeper understanding of the kind of people they are. I know some excellent people.

I remember worrying if we had invited anyone to the house after the service. Somehow the word got out, and when I got home, my house was almost full. My family had jumped in to serve food, make coffee, and answer the door. At some point, the flowers from the funeral home arrived, and I tried to point out where to put them. Others jumped in, and all of that just happened the way it needed to happen. I will never forget that feeling. I was standing in the home that we had built together, the home we had planned to stay in until retirement, to say goodbye to him. I stood on the exact tile where I had the premonition that I'd lose him, and I looked around at all the things we had loved and laughed about designing.

There was the Christmas tree nook because, for Jayson, all homes were created around where a Christmas tree would go. There was the prom staircase. He had been so excited about looking forward to taking pictures of our daughters in their prom dresses on the curving staircase. There would be no more Christmases with him, and I'd be the only one seeing those sweet girls off to their prom. I could hear the conversations all around me, yet what I wanted was to lie in my bed and wrap myself in silence and solitude.

We were out of coffee. Suddenly that became an essential issue to me. I had put out the percolator, which was my tried and true coffee pot over the years, and someone had made a second pot that came out weak. I took it upon myself to fuss over that issue and tried to fix it. I'm not sure why I didn't do what I knew needed to be done — the heating plate required to be cooled down before starting a new pot. But I never even thought to do that. I was overcome with anger that something would happen to make this time less than perfect. But how could it be perfect without him there? He would have loved a house full of people. He would have loved that I was taking care of all the little details. It always made him so proud to host a gathering. We hadn't had the chance to do that since having children. Between busy work schedules and parenting, we still had not gotten our social footing. We designed this house to entertain again, but this would probably be the last large gathering it would see and he wasn't here to enjoy it.

We tend to think of endings as final punctuations on events. We think of them as immediate and absolute. What I've learned is that endings can be long. That service, that reception, that day marked the beginning of the end for me. It was the beginning of the unraveling of everything I had worked for and everything I had achieved. It was the beginning of a journey of letting go and a journey of accepting. I could no longer have the life for which I had worked so hard. That was hard enough to bear on its own, but what has been even harder to accept is that what life has left in front of me is unknown. I no longer know what I'm trying to build. Is there such a thing as an endless ending?

4

I Have News

In my mind, it would only take a short while to take care of all of the loose ends. I was, after all, a certified project manager. Scandinavian efficiency was in my genes. Little did I know the difficulties that lay before me in simply trying to give people money, settle accounts, and close accounts no longer needed. To say that other people made it complicated would be an understatement. Everything I did seemed to require knowledgeable navigation and even diplomacy. It was taxing. I wanted time to grieve. I wanted time to just be with my family. But the loose ends wait for no one, and I learned many of the voices behind the bills didn't care.

As I've said, we were planners. We had planned for the event of our deaths long before we knew that one of us would be lost sooner rather than later. I knew where every account was and the balance of every asset. My name was on just about everything it could be. We had designed everything to be straightforward and easily administered in the event one of us died. Our planning wasn't the problem. The web of medical bills I had to unravel was insane. They were not only myriad but also untimely and often inaccurate. It fell to me to set them straight.

I remember taking a stack of bills and putting them in order of due date. I decided to start with the first bill and work my way through them to the end. I had created my list of questions to ask to be sure that I had accurate information from which to settle the accounts. I would ask:

1. Is this the most current balance on the account?

2. Are there any charges that have not yet been posted to the account?

3. Can we verify the insurance information to be sure that you have the correct insurer?

4. Has insurance paid or authorized payment on any part of the outstanding balance?

5. Can you generate electronic copies of any future bills or statements to ensure that I can catalog them and close out the accounts once they have been settled?

It seemed easy in my mind. Of course, it was anything but easy. I called the number on the first bill. There was a long and complicated phone tree that I had to navigate before getting to a live human. The live human answered, "*mumbles.*"

"This is Jakob Franzen. I'm sorry. I didn't catch your name"

"*Mumbles.*"

"Um, okay. I'm calling to inquire about my late husband's account," I said, trying to be gracious and cooperative.

"Sir, there is an outstanding balance on that account." She sounded indignant.

"Yes, I'm aware of that. My husband passed away just last month. So I'm only now getting to the outstanding bills. I have some questions so that I can be sure I pay it properly." I continued to try to be cooperative. After all, I did want to pay the bill so that the account could be closed.

"Sir, are you prepared to pay that balance today?" She was now insistent and impatient.

"Not until I've asked my questions." My tone was a bit sharper.

"Sir, please don't get an attitude with me. You owe the money, and I won't be treated like that." She was now defiant and offended.

"I'm not trying to get an attitude; I'm trying to get clarity on the bill so that I can pay it." I was trying to calm my voice as much as I could.

"Sir, the bill is clear. You owe the balance." She had dropped all professionalism.

"Is there someone else I can speak with?" I thought perhaps a fresh start with someone new would be more productive.

"No. You'll have to call back later." Dial tone.

What had gone so wrong? Nothing that happened in that entire exchange had been my intention. She knocked the wind out of my sails, and I just couldn't bring myself to dial that number again. That's when I created a new folder. This new folder would be for bills that needed extra courage to address. The thing that stood out to me most about this particular call, and I remember it well because it was the first of many, was that the person on the other end of the phone at no point acknowledged my loss. Her focus was purely on the money. Having worked in human resources for over 30 years, I knew that our insurance plan would pay most of what was on that bill as a covered service. I also knew I had money set aside to take care of deductibles, co-pays, and outstanding balances for items that weren't covered. I was lucky. Yet, she treated me as if I were going to try to get out of paying the bill. She treated me as if I were going to try to pull something over on her. She treated me less than human. She wasn't the last to do that.

I began to wonder, did she lack compassion, or was she just never taught that she should have empathy for other human beings? Death can make people uncomfortable. When we experience death as children, many look to the adults around us and emulate their responses. It's how we learn to express our grief. In many circles, there is specific etiquette to suffering and dealing with the grieving that we're taught. What happens when as children, the adults around us are broken? What happens when we don't have anyone to watch handle grief healthily? All we walk away with is that grief is uncomfortable, whether it's our own or someone else's. We learn to avoid those things that make us uncomfortable.

I have no way of knowing if this is what happened to the woman on the phone. But what I do know is that she never once acknowledged the fact that my husband had died. Her only focus was on the money that I owed for his treatment. I wonder if it ever crossed her mind that it would be kinder to acknowledge my loss and then walk me through my questions? As it turned out, I had many more similar conversations. The people on the other end of the phone were younger and probably had not experienced much in the way of grief. Their job was to get accounts closed and bills paid. They tended to stick with the script and unfortunately compassion and kindness were not included. The human element was completely nonexistent I'm not sure if they realized or ever knew that they were passing up a chance to be genuinely human.

As I went about my tasks taking care of hospital bills and orienting myself to all of the other obligations we had, I had to call the county tax assessor's office. I wondered what that call would hold? Many government offices don't have the best reputation for customer service. While I'm sure that is an unfair assessment of many, it was the perception I had in my head at the time. Our house was new, and this was the first year property taxes would be due. Jayson always took care of that detail, and he had still taken care of many things on his good days while he sat in bed. Now, it was my turn. I dialed the number, and I braced myself for what was to come.

"Hi, I'm calling because my husband passed away last month, and I need to confirm whether or not our property taxes have been paid and whether or not a homestead form has been submitted." I could hear the silence on the other end of the phone. The woman who had answered was taking a deep breath. I was unsure how this conversation was going to go.

"Sir, I am so sorry for your loss. I recently lost my father-in-law. I can only imagine what you have to go through right now. I know there is nothing I can say, but I can certainly help you with this and make sure everything is up-to-date."

"Thank you." At that moment, she had made a connection with me. She acknowledged my loss and disclosed one of her own. She highlighted that we were both a part of the human experience, and she took a minute to see me — to really see me and show empathy for what I must have been feeling at that precise moment. It surprised me. The funny thing is that it shouldn't have.

Shouldn't our default be a meaningful connection? As we have progressed further and further down the path of human development and the embrace of technology, we have begun to lose sight of some of the most critical aspects of the social nature of our species. We don't have to know each other to react with kindness or the understanding of similar experiences. I will probably never talk to the woman again, but in a few brief seconds, she made me feel like I wasn't alone.

Settling accounts, dealing with bills, and changing the names on services were only a tiny part of what I had to do. I had tried to make sure that I let everyone know when Jayson died. It's funny how "everyone" can be subjective. We had a particular circle of friends who, of course, knew when it happened. Thanks to social media, I had access to friends of his that we didn't share. But which ones of them were close enough to him to tell? He was never very active on social media. I couldn't be sure who had been "friended" out of convenience and who was someone he had known for a while.

Trying to compose some sort of announcement for social media was daunting. It would be a post most people would see so it couldn't be jarring. It had to be proper. I had to convey the message with the right tone, but there was always the chance that someone would be offended because I didn't tell them personally. Some people hate to find out essential things on social media. But in reality, it would have been impossible for me to let everyone know personally. Some of our closest friends had to be told by other close friends simply because I didn't have the strength to tell the story over and over and go through the same emotional whirlwind every time. Everyone seemed to understand.

I created the post and made it both public and shareable. I hoped that those who knew of other friends or acquaintances would share it so that the news would travel. The announcement included his memorial service time and location. I wanted those who knew him to be able to come and to pay their respects if they chose to do so.

One morning, sitting at my desk, it occurred that there were probably people in our neighborhood who should be told. Jayson was more social than I was, and he would often talk to our new neighbors while he walked to the mailboxes or walked our oldest daughter to school. There were times after we moved in that he would want to do something with the lawn or the flowerbeds despite the oxygen concentrator he had to wear. I had no idea who he had gotten to know in the short eight months we had been here and who he hadn't.

Luckily we have a neighborhood email group. We're a small enclave of about only 30 houses, and so the list was short. I decided I'd use that email address list to let people know that he had died, especially those who knew him. But how do you start an email like that? I sat there, at my computer, watching a blinking cursor on the email. I finally typed the subject, "Memorial Services for Jayson." In the body of the email, I shared that the girls and I were heartbroken by the loss and that we welcomed anyone who wanted to attend the memorial service.

The response was emotionally overwhelming. These were people I barely knew, but they took the time to respond to my email to send their condolences and offer their support. These people, many of whom I'd only waved to on the street, were expressing how sorry they were that I had lost my husband and my best friend. The neighborhood is diverse, comprised of older couples, young families, and people from a variety of cultures. Everyone jumped in, and everyone made an effort to connect.

The many reactions I received in the wake of Jayson's death caused me to think, "How could those reactions be so different?" Grief makes us uncomfortable, but do we have to stay in that place of discomfort? I had seen people choose to avoid acknowledging it at all so that they could awkwardly sidestep having to make the connection, and then some embraced the moment. There were those who took a minute to see the grief, make a connection, and share their moments as if to say, "We're the same! You're not in this alone."

So many of us don't want to face our mortality. We would like to think that life continues to march onward, unimpeded. There would always be another Christmas, another Hanukkah, more Thanksgivings, more birthdays, and weddings in a perfect world. In our minds, we would attend all of these events whole, youthful, and sound. That's not the way life works. We age. Our minds age and change as we grow older, but our bodies show more visible signs of change. I often walk through my bathroom and glance into the mirror at an unfamiliar body and face that looks more like my grandfather looked every day. These are the normal pathways of aging. Sadly, disease can derail our aging, both mentally and physically.

To cope, many of us make jokes about getting older. We joke about the struggles of losing weight, the battles of staying in shape, and the onset of presbyopia, farsightedness. I have reading glasses stashed all around the house. My mind still feels the same as it did when I was in my twenties. The mental picture of myself is of me in my twenties. My mind is wiser — or at least I hope it is — from all of the experiences I've had in the 30 years beyond my twenties. However, when I look in the mirror, I have an unrealistic expectation of what I will see. Ultimately there is a moment of disappointment when the man in the mirror is aging, heavier, with gray in his hair, and puffiness under his eyes. He looks tired.

We're all headed to an ultimate demise, but we don't seem to want to talk about that. Culturally there isn't enough dialogue about experiencing aging. We think about how we will get as much as possible out of life more than where we will be stashed as we get older — as if getting older means that we must belong to some separate community and be kept out of the youthful zeal of the mainstream. Sometimes it feels like our society is trying to dim the lights before turning them out for good.

The psychology behind how we think of death seems to be at play in every conversation you have when you lose someone. The whole process of settling accounts left me tired and constantly trying to refine some sort of explanation of why I was calling and what had happened to my husband. Why did there need to be such a lengthy explanation? My husband had died, and I needed to take care of business. The saddest part to me was the lack of empathy for what I must have been feeling. There was usually so much discomfort on the other end of the phone and an effort to bring the conversation to a close as quickly as possible. Wouldn't it have been better if, somewhere along the way, these people had been shown how to open up their minds and simply witness the grief of someone else?

Awkward conversations were almost always on tap, even in the realms outside of trying to pay bills and close accounts. There were people I worked with and people I only ever saw casually. Every time I would run into someone, I would think to myself, "I wonder if they know?" If they didn't know, I had to try to figure out some way to tell them or did I? "Hey, my husband died," isn't an easy comment to work into a conversation. Sometimes I would even lose my focus on what someone was saying to me as I tried to pay countless numbers of scenarios out in my head.

Sometimes, after holding my breath in terror, I would find a way to utter the phrase. This utterance was typically met with shock and then followed up with sadness. I found that so many people are uncomfortable with the words "he died." They prefer some softer phrase of "he passed" or "he passed away." The truth of the matter is that his human form died. It has ceased to exist, and my daughters and I have suffered a traumatic loss because of it. Maybe we all need to be more truthful and clear about what happens in death. Sure, everyone has some idea of what it means to have a soul and what happens to the soul when the body dies, but the universal experience in death is that the body dies. The person we have known and loved is gone and is not coming back. Regardless of our ideas about the soul or where it goes, the vessel that anchored them here is gone.

I think I was always the most taken back by people who wanted to change the subject quickly. They didn't want to know how I was doing, despite uttering those very words as a question. They were at a loss of what to say and how to engage. I had looked them in the eye and told them I had experienced a trauma, and they looked away. One of the healthiest things to do is to talk about it. To talk about it with those around us makes it real and seen. It validates our feelings of loss and makes us feel connected to the greater human collective. Our pain is witnessed.

But in those days after Jayson's death, I would encounter person after person who looked away. They didn't want to see my pain or understand my loss. It was as if they were afraid it would somehow taint them to know it or understand it. Perhaps it's just that they were taught that it's impolite to speak of such things as it may bring up pain for the person who experienced the loss or they simply lacked the emotional intelligence — empathy — to be able to talk about it with compassion, kindness and a loving heart. Or, maybe they did not know what to say because they weren't taught how to talk about death and how to handle one's emotions and be able to relate to the person who has suffered a major loss in their lives. It is possible that out of fear of saying the wrong thing and feeling inappropriate, they didn't say anything at all and emotionally they shut down. Death is a delicate subject and for some people it's easier to turn their heads around, look the other way and not say anything because they don't want to be face their own emotions revolving around death as it may trigger a major loss in their own lives. However, whatever it was that made them feel that it was best to ignore the conversation, I would counter with the fact that there is always a socially delicate way to engage complex topics. It usually begins with kindness and authenticity. Empathy conveys the message, "I see you." And isn't that what anyone who is grieving wants?

My social calendar was never a full one — except for events for my daughters. I had become the typical "parent taxi" taking them to piano lessons, scouting meetings, playdates, and birthday parties. But in the months after Jayson's death, my world was quieter. People kept their distance. I'm not sure if they thought it was appropriate to give me space or if they just thought I'd be too sad to have around at gatherings. It's clearer to me now that I look back on it because, at the time, I had made the poor decision to take a new job. The job would keep me too busy to join in on anything social. I was, after all, trying to learn to balance being a single parent and working.

If there is anything I could say to any of the people who kept their distance at the time, I think I'd tell them I would have benefitted more from them being more aggressive. Looking back, I would have liked the opportunity to say no to social invitations, but I would have also enjoyed the chance to say yes. I may not have realized it much at the time, but I had an inner need to be seen by others. Not just seen for who I was but for what I was experiencing. Some of the best encounters were of those I'd see who would simply look me in the eye and say, "I'm so sorry Jayson died." Their acknowledgment and compassion were some of the most useful expressions I experienced. It taught me an important lesson about how to treat others who had experienced loss. It is our responsibility to bear witness to the grief of our fellow human beings. The other thing I learned during this time was that I would be more alone in this than I ever imagined.

The latter was a key piece of knowledge for me as I later thought through what could be different. I often think through these things as advice I would give, even though no one is asking. Loneliness is a huge part of losing a spouse. For me, I'm fortunate to have young children who keep me busy and offer a company that brings me both — joy and often laughter. I'm also well designed for solitude. I get my energy from quiet time alone. But, after 16 years with someone who was always there, ready to hear every thought, every opinion, and help resolve every problem, I felt lonely. Loneliness is peculiar. I wasn't lonely for just any company, but his specifically. There was nothing quite like the time that we were together. We fit together so well. There was never really a need for one to change to accommodate the other. Sure, there was a compromise, but we grew together along the same path by and large.

While I don't think anyone, in particular, could have eased this specific loneliness, the opportunity for so many people to witness what I was feeling was entirely missed by so many. In every instance when I made a phone call to settle a bill, when I ran into someone in the store, when I sat next to someone at a meeting, or even when I talked to another parent at a birthday party, there was the opportunity to look me in the eye and acknowledge my loss. It was an opportunity to remind me that I was part of the human collective and seen. Instead, I spent so much time feeling awkward and broken because I no longer fit what everyone expected.

Things would be so different if we all changed how we respond to someone who begins any exchange with "I lost my spouse." That should be a flag for any of us to be quiet, present, and fully engaged. Whatever it is that we need to talk about next can wait. If we're on the other end of the phone and about to discuss a balance due or an account that needs to be closed, we can take just a minute to hear and "see" the person on the other end of the line without feeling threatened in any way shape or form. Life doesn't revolve around account balances. Yes, it's important to just take a minute to understand what's going on with a fellow human being and to put ourselves aside to be able to at least acknowledge and accept that at that particular moment, life isn't about us but about someone else. It's about the irreplaceable loss that another human being is experiencing and about coming to the understanding that we are all human beings and that we're here to support each other. We may or may not have many mundane things in common, if any, with strangers or with people close to us, but as human beings there are at least two constant elements that we all have in common — life and death. The emotions attached to these two elements don't change, as much as we might try, and our personal and professional work environment does not affect them. They're constant — they're there all the time. They're a part of our existence.

Work is no different. So many people return to work before it's time and try to wear a brave face around the office or over videoconferences. They get caught up in this idea that they need to be moving on, especially where work is concerned. Many workplaces only offer four days of bereavement leave for the loss of a spouse. It sends the message that this is all the time that you need to recover. All the while, it is far from it. Co-workers avoid talking to them about the loss because it's not appropriate for the workplace in their minds or it's a distraction to the grieving person. The avoidance of their experience contributes to their feelings of isolation and loneliness. They begin to feel less and less seen as a whole person.

There is a lot of talk these days around showing up to work as a whole person. That message resonates with a workforce who has long tried to balance work with a life that had to remain unseen. But when we ask someone to show up as a whole person to work, we have to be ready to receive them as a whole person. We can't just simply nod at whatever is going on in their life and move on. We all work better when we know that we're seen when we're acknowledged and appreciated as the whole person we are.

I often find myself imagining teaching a class on how to react to a grieving person. That may seem pretentious, but it's borne out of a desire to help others understand what they can say and do to make it a more gracious exchange when they encounter someone who is grieving. So many awkward and disastrous encounters lead me to believe that we don't talk about grief enough. It would seem that we have a very narrow idea of what grief should be and that when things don't fit in that little box, we toss box and all. We need to open our minds to what grief can be in general and specifically for what grief may be for those we know — the grieving need to know that their grief is valid.

There is no one-way to deal with grief because we all grieve differently. But there is a way to acknowledge it that can transcend how a person is grieving. See them. When you feel the urge to be uncomfortable and back away, embrace that discomfort and lean into it. Let the grieving person cry and wail if they need to do so. Let them experience their feelings and emotions in whatever way is right for them, even though none of it may be suitable for you. By bearing witness to their grief, you're sending a message that they are not broken. They are human and a part of everything human.

The next time you encounter someone who has lost someone close to them, take some time to be present for them. Don't offer advice. Don't say it gets better. After all, you can't know that. Just simply acknowledge them and bear witness to what they're feeling. If they are someone you know and will see again, don't do it just once. Do it any time they need it. They'll tell you if they need some space from it, but you'll help them feel connected and cared for by another human being.

We can't sweep death under the rug. It is our common destination. Some of us will age slowly toward it, while others will be taken from their lives far too soon. While none of us want to fixate on our impending demise, we shouldn't shy away from talking about it either. Talking about how we prepare for our death and the loss of others can help us have better conversations later when we do lose someone.   Being able to have those conversations and knowing that our feelings about loss are valid, will help us establish our resilience. When we understand death as a part of life, we realize that it is only a part and that there will be more life to live even after losing someone close to us.

5

Bereavement Leave

Jayson's death wasn't abrupt, though the onset of his illness was. He was sick for about a year before he died. I watched him have good days and bad days until the bad days outnumbered the good days. He found ways to shore himself up to work, and I took on more and more of caring for him and life at home. The timing, for when he could no longer work, coincided with the time I was interviewing for a new job and preparing for the inevitable exit from my current role. The holidays were also upon us, but he was in no shape to travel. Days usually filled with family, laughter, and a house full of food were oddly quiet. I did my best to create traditional meals and to hold things together for our girls. He was rarely hungry, and with so few of us, I had to keep those meals small, despite his grand recipe requests like the Cornish game hens for Christmas dinner.

We didn't know at the time that those were our last days and our last holidays as a family. He struggled to sit on the hearth of the fireplace to exchange gifts at Christmastime as he watched our girls open their presents with excitement. I just thought we were only in the bad days. In my heart, I hoped that he would be better and that we would have more time. I didn't realize that we were already on the downward slope of his demise, but he was present. He was smiling. He was kissing and hugging our daughters and making memories for them. I was capturing them in pictures. I sometimes wonder if I would have done it any differently if I had known. I wonder whether I would have taken more photos or posed more moments, had I known this would be our last Christmas together. Would I have just been too sad to capture any of it? We sometimes think that if we had the gift of foresight, we would do things right and avoid mistakes or poor choices. I don't think we can ever really know how we would react to the burden of knowing.

My days at the end of that year were filled with the work of my current job and peppered with interviews for a new job. Jayson's were filled with struggle and medical procedures. He had to be hospitalized for one procedure, and I remember taking an interview call while we were there. It was an interesting sensation to be talking to someone on the phone and trying to keep your voice upbeat and your energy up, all while surrounded by sickness and uncertainty. That day was such a gray and cold Texas winter day. I remember walking around in my pea coat as I passed in and out of the hospital, hoping to find pockets of quiet so that my conversation wasn't interrupted. As I look back on that day now, it was a day filled with an incredible amount of stress because my job, whether my current one or a new one, had suddenly become much more important to us. As Jayson became unable to work, I would become our sole provider.

We had always done such a great job as a team. Even before we had children, we found a great rhythm in managing our money and taking care of each other. We had started as many couples do. We each kept our own money and contributed to a joint account to pay for living expenses and housing. That later quickly flipped when we realized we'd gain so much more by pooling our money and each of us drawing an allowance off of the account. We both roughly made the same salaries, so it felt equitable.

My job roles tended to be in the tech sector and were a little less stable, so pooling our money allowed us to make long-term plans that would allow for the hiccups that I usually experienced. Our strategy worked better than we expected. Life became a series of achieved financial goals. That stability is what put us in a place to create our family. That stability helped our family flourish. That stability was now in jeopardy. I was filled with doubt as I wondered if I could do it on my own. I remember thinking, "At least I'll have him as a sounding board. We can still set the strategy together." I didn't know at the time that I was about to lose that too.

Interviewing for a professional role is often a process of hurrying up and waiting. As interviewers are available, there is a rush to schedule you with the next person in the line-up. As interviews are completed, the company retreats to debrief and begin figuring out who's next. When that takes place in the last couple of months of the year, it gets even more difficult. People start to take extended time away connected to the holidays. The year slows down, and everyone wants time with family and friends. The new company I was talking to wasn't any different, and as a long-time Human Resources practitioner, I understood the process and wasn't in any hurry. The gaps in conversations were welcomed because I needed that space to care for my husband. He required so much more help just getting around, and I had to make sure our daughters had what they needed as well. As the days grew even shorter, my time with my family grew greater. We cocooned as school let out for winter break and stayed inside around a roaring fire. I don't think I could have planned it any better had I known what was coming. Maybe my brain has already started to soften those memories. I'm three years out from those days as I write this. But time did seem to slow down. We all got more time together, and the hectic schedules of work and school gave way to the slowness and the warmth of holiday family time.

During that time, Jayson and I were able to have a long, in-depth conversation about what life might look like without him. We double-checked wills, reviewed life insurance policies, and discussed strategies that I might take if left on my own. I both loved and hated those talks. They were a way to reiterate that we were on the same page and that all of the planning work we did before having children was standing the test of time. I hated them because they set loose a flurry of whispers in my mind that I was losing him. I went through so many fits of disbelief and anger. I held on to every last shred of hope that he would be okay. I hoped that he would be with us for just a few more years — long enough to see his girls begin to blossom into beautiful young women. I wanted him to be here long enough to know that I could do this on my own. So that he would have the peace to know things were left in good hands. The anxiety and the doubt of the uncertainty at not knowing how long he would last were crippling. Little did I know that we would only have less than six weeks left at that point.

There were plans and contingency plans with the new job and plans if the new job didn't pan out. We looked near term, long term, and even mid-term. He felt sure his time was short. I felt confident I didn't want to let him go no matter where it may fall on that timeline. He had another hospital stay on the evening of Christmas day. Fortunately, he was home for New Year's Eve, and we rang in the new year early. I held on to a bit of hope that things still might get better. Even with him sick, we had pulled off a good Christmas. He ordered toys for our girls from the bed; I ensured they were assembled and ready to go for Christmas morning. We had two sweet, happy little girls, and that was always our goal. I clung to their smiles and their joy and hoped that would be enough for me for the new year.

The offer for the new job came just after I returned to work. It was exciting because, on the surface, it was a job I had always wanted. It was the right level. It had global responsibility, and it was going to provide challenges in all the ways I wanted to be challenged as a professional. It didn't take me long to review the offer with Jayson, talk about how the new job would work, and then communicate my acceptance back to the organization. I gave notice to my current employer, settled on a start date with the new employer, and began the work of wrapping my role so that I'd be ready to move on. It was in those days that Jayson started to decline. I had to work from home during the last week of my old job just so that I could take care of him. My employer at the time was incredibly generous in that regard. No matter what, family came first for them, and their actions proved that time and again.

I was just a week out from starting my new job when Jayson died. As that tragedy played out, I panicked. I was in the gray area between jobs. How was my income going to look? Would I need to push my start date out? Would they let me move my start date out? The questions were myriad. When you lose your spouse, you don't yet fully appreciate how life is going to look. Your pressured responses are similar to those you would have under other stressful circumstances. I remember thinking that I couldn't lose this new job. It was necessary so that I could take care of my girls and continue to provide for them. I hadn't even thought about life insurance at that point or how that might look. I just knew I needed to begin working as soon as I could. After several conversations with my new employer, I agreed to push my start date out by a couple more weeks.

In my mind, I thought that being busy would be the best thing for me, and starting a new role at a new company would be a busy time. I justified it with the fact that Jayson would want me to get things moving again and not waste time. But I had no idea, and he would certainly not have had any idea of what is required after the trauma of loss. I now know that I took steps in a direction that wasn't healthy for me and stunted my ability to heal. I prolonged my trauma by trying to get back to a life that wasn't ever going to be the same.

As an HR professional, I'd spent my fair share of time writing policy. Leave policies used to be so important to organizations because the accounting of time, it was believed, translated to better profits if that time was managed correctly. There was, of course, paid time off, which made up the core of an employee's leave allowance. There were also statutory holidays and those little extra days that an employer could throw in there to be more competitive. But then there were those allotments of time that were created without a whole lot of forethought and simply added to the list based on competitive research and survey data. There was time for jury duty, short-term disability, family and medical leave, and of course, bereavement leave. Some of those categories provided short-term pay and others provided protected leave but with no compensation. Bereavement was often divided up into different amounts based on the familial relationship with the deceased. There was absolutely no attention paid to the fact that some of us create families outside the traditional structure. For some of us, losing a close friend is much more traumatic than losing an estranged relative.

Bereavement is an odd term. Its typical definition is a "state of being sad." When used in terms of paid leave, the assumption is that it is a state of being sad. It's a time to participate in the religious rituals surrounding death, and taking care of any necessary formalities. The average time awarded as paid leave for such actives where a spouse is concerned is four days. Looking back on that now, I find it crass that I didn't speak up more to request more time. How can anyone take care of the overwhelming number of tasks required when a spouse dies and prepare to get back to work in four days? I'll never forget a conversation I had with a CEO when I suggested we change bereavement leave to a two-week block. His response was to simply allow employees to take their vacation time if they needed more time. Looking back, my response now to that statement is much more visceral than it was at the time. Grieving is not a vacation.

There are many studies on the efficacy of time and work, especially related to the 40-hour workweek. Born out of industrialism, this arbitrary work schedule has been with us for almost 100 years. Studies have shown that working longer or more hours doesn't necessarily increase productivity but that also reducing the number of hours worked in a week doesn't decrease productivity either. I find those studies fascinating, but what always intrigued me was how a company reacted to the significant changes in an employee's life. I was always eager to figure out the disparity between parental leave in the US and parental leave in Europe. I typically had to devote pages and pages to how parental leave was handled among countries for a global organization. Everything was always set to do the statutory minimum for each country. I often wondered what would happen if we took the richest of the plans and made that plan the corporate standard across countries.

When an employee welcomes a child into their lives, whether it's by birth, surrogacy, adoption, or any other means available for family building, their whole life changes, and their employer gets a chance to be part of that and support them in that milestone. But what about the milestones that death brings? Employers also have an opportunity to be there for their employees when they lose someone close to them. They have a chance to bear witness to that loss, to embrace their employee, and help them through the trauma of grief and loss. Yet, most prefer to keep grief and bereavement at a distance. They send a plant or flowers to the funeral. They provide a few days away to take care of things. Then they expect that their employee is back and ready to move on after their loss in just a few days.

I had the luxury of giving myself more time. I didn't realize it at the time, but I also had the luxury of declining the offer and taking the time I needed to heal. Amid all the trauma, all the flurry of funeral homes, memorial services, and insurance policies, it's easy to lose your focus and your train of thought. I took a couple of extra weeks for myself. I honestly thought that would be enough to get everything to focus on a new job and keep myself busy. I couldn't have been more wrong. Whether it's four days or four weeks, none of that is enough time for anyone to catch their breath and figure out what life looks like after losing a spouse. We're primed to think about fresh starts after loss. The idea is romanticized, and we're drawn to the concept of a clean slate. In popular culture we see television shows and movies that depict a person believed to be strong and able to begin to move forward after only six months, and suddenly their life miraculously turns around.

But one of the most important things I've learned is that you have to be ready for that fresh start whenever it may come. I wasn't at all prepared. I still don't know what this life is supposed to look like at almost three years in. After all this time, I'm still playing it by ear every single day. Maybe the time is different for everyone, but I know now that a year would have been best for me to take time away and to adjust. Some other widowers I've spoken with have wished they had been able to take six months. Everyone's circumstance is different, but none of it seems to fit in four neat days.

The return to work is just as hard. For me, it was a return to work in general and the start of a new role with a new company. I had lots to learn. I had to learn a whole new set of executives, a new group of employees, understand an existing culture and figure out what strategies were in place and what I needed to craft or re-invent. When a grieving person returns to the workplace, it's so essential that their grief be acknowledged. But grief makes us uncomfortable. We don't like to talk about it; we don't like to hear about it from others. So we pretend that the polite thing to do is not address it all. Discussions of loss are relegated to the category of inappropriate topics for the workplace. I would argue there could be no better topic for someone who has experienced loss. Those of us who grieve need to be seen.

When I started my new job, I was asked if I wanted people to avoid the conversation or if it was okay to talk to me about it. I was so impressed that someone would actually take the time to ask me that question. Yes, yes, I wanted to talk about it! What an excellent opportunity for people to get to know me and understand where I was coming from in this post-loss life. Yet oddly, that was the last discussion of my loss. No one ever wanted to talk about it. I was suddenly standing in the middle of eggshells, and no one wanted to walk across those. I think I would have been able to clarify better how my grief was affecting my work, if I had talked about it more. I would have probably understood my fit or lack thereof better, if I could articulate what I was feeling and how I experienced what was happening in the workday. In looking back, maybe I could have done more to encourage those conversations and probably should have. Instead, I began to feel more isolated from my peers and became more and more out of touch with the work I needed to be doing. Finally, on a cold day in January, we all decided to call it quits almost a year to the day. Hindsight tells me that it should have never really started in the first place.

How could I have made such a colossal mistake? After all, I'm a professional with 30 years of HR experience. I should have seen the signs, but I was blinded by my grief when I chose to move forward, which ended up not being forward at all. The job, and everything that it was, would have been perfect for me as a husband and father. I would have gone into it very differently, and I think ultimately been much more successful. But what I didn't realize at the time was that for a recently widowed man trying to figure out life with two small children, that job was a terrible fit. Because I couldn't see that, I kept trying and failing and never could figure out why I couldn't make it work.

I don't think I'm alone. I think many of us question our jobs as we return to them after a loss. We should. In all of the free-flowing advice that we get after a loss, no one bothers to tell you that you're about to become a completely different person. Not only did your spouse die, but the person you were while you were with them died too. Grief, like an onion, has many layers of loss. In the beginning, we're grieving the loss of the person we loved. In time, we find that we're grieving so many other things in our lives that were attached to that person. No longer was I the person who could travel between countries on short notice, hold space for employee issues, or design complex, multinational compensation plans. My attention was needed elsewhere. I had two little girls who needed their Papa much more than any foreign or domestic office needed me. I didn't realize that was what was pulling my focus for far too long. Leaving was best for the organization I had joined and me. I needed to be something different — someone different. My path had changed. It just took me some extra time to realize it.

On a flight home from New York on a cold winter morning, I contemplated what life would look like now that I was headed out on my own. I wanted to feel sad or remorseful. After all, I was leaving a job that, on the outside, was the job I had always wanted. But, it had become a job that I did not need. It pulled me away from my children, and despite what it offered us in security, my girls were missing out on the thing they needed most. They needed me. They needed to be able to spend time with me. They didn't need me using FaceTime from another country. They didn't need me spending over an hour each way commuting the 20 miles into the local office. They didn't need me picking them up from after-care in a frazzled and exhausted state. None of this worked, and it took me far too long to see it. As I watched the clouds sneak by me, an insignificant dot racing across the sky, I realized that none of it mattered anymore to me. That path was over, and I would never fully achieve what I had hoped to, but now I no longer wanted to achieve it. I had to do something else.

I can only really describe the feeling I was left with as terror. At my age, life is really about enjoying the apex of your career. It's about finding that thing that is the capstone. I was leaving that behind. My purpose was different now; my legacy wouldn't be in business. My legacy had to be in my children. But, of course, I was still going to have to provide for them. I had to pursue a business that would allow me much more time to be present with them and build up our finances so that they didn't have to struggle. In some ways, it all felt like a weighty burden. Little whispers of self-doubt began. I wondered if I was going to be able to do right by them. Only time would be able to tell. New York was behind me, Austin was ahead of me, and fear was in my chest. My entire life was about to be different.

I wonder, sometimes, how often do we overlook the monumental changes someone has to make after a loss? There is this sort of expectation that they'll get back to life as usual. That they'll get back to the job they had before life was interrupted. After all, we liked them just the way they were. It would be uncomfortable for us if they were to change. What we should do is allow them room to ask the redefining questions. "Does this job still suit me?" or "Does this job still fit my family?" The key is that we don't hold those answers for them. Only they do. Only they can know what it is that they need to do. Sometimes, those plans are an absolute mistake, but they need the room to make those mistakes. Our job is to be there for them should they fall and support them as they try. Of course, our job is also to take part in the sweet celebration when they succeed.

We also have to understand that they are going through yet another kind of grief. They may have liked who they were in their career. In my case, I wanted to be where I had ended up in my career. There had certainly been plenty of fits and starts, but I was finally getting to a point where I liked my level and my ability to influence an organization. Losing my husband changed all of that. I was unable to focus or devote the time necessary to make all of that work. I had to let it go, and it wasn't quick or easy. It took me a year to admit it and realize that path no longer lies before me. I'm sure that things are a little easier for some people, and the process can be that much harder for others. The point is that none of this happens if we're crowding the grieving and not giving them room to breathe. In the noise of our advice, they don't get the chance to listen to their hearts.

I guess once an HR professional, always an HR professional because I still toy with the idea of what I would change in the workplace related to grief. I certainly like the idea of giving more time. Ultimately, losing someone close to you is a change in how you define your family. I would mirror the leave available for other family changes and offer up to 12 weeks away from work. In addition, I would suggest a modified schedule for up to 12 weeks upon return that allows for taking care of any loose ends. I can attest to the fact that there can be quite a few. Moreover, I would have an HR team create a process for reintegration into the workplace. The job an employee held before losing someone close might not be the right fit for them and their new family

71

circumstance once they return back to work. Yet, their talent and skill may still be the right fit for the organization. Through regular sessions with an HR business partner and a therapist, an employee could find the ideal job fit. It may very well be the job they've held, or it could be some new iteration. I like the idea of giving someone the chance to evolve and supporting them in that evolution rather than watching them leave and grow somewhere else.

There is so much we have to learn in the workplace. We are human. We don't have the luxury of checking that quality at the door when we arrive at work. It's funny to say that I have seen a lot of change in the workplace. I don't feel that old. Yet, I've been in the workforce for over 30 years. When I first started, I remember being counseled by a more senior colleague not to ever talk about my personal life at work. She told me it was unprofessional, and as professionals, we should keep personal challenges out of sight at work. Back then I also wore a suit to work and carried a briefcase.

Today, we are so much more integrated into our work. When I was in an actual office, I knew who had children playing minor league, selling Girl Scout Cookies, and getting ready for a big senior year of high school. We've learned it's okay to know these things. We've learned that it's okay to show up as a whole person. Grief shouldn't be any different. It happens to all of us and shouldn't only be talked about in whispers. We are constantly growing, changing, and evolving. That is part of who we are as humans. When we experience loss, the changes that transpire thereafter are accelerated. How we work and what we do for a living can suddenly be called into question. As bystanders of grief, I think we need to allow the space for that to happen, bear witness to it, and support our grieving friends in their search for redefined meaning in their work. We get to participate in their resilience.

6

Forging a New Path

When you decide to go out and start your own business, the field is big, bright, and terrifying. It's wide open and full of opportunity -— and failure. This is not my first time starting a business. I did it twice before, and I was relatively successful. One iteration of me as an entrepreneur had me traveling all over the country to consult on leveraging HR technology for better HR practice. My second iteration had me working with companies on HR strategy. Neither venture into business on my own had been intended to be permanent. Both of those ventures were designed as a means to an end. They gave me more profound experience that allowed me to be a more strategic HR executive, even though most organizations prefer tactical HR.

This time was different and was even scarier to me. I was unsure of which direction I wanted to go when I made my decision. My primary objective was to do something that allowed me to be more present for my children. Traveling was definitely out of the question. They needed me. They had just lost their Daddy the year before, and I had been gone much of that year. However, the more daunting challenge was that I needed to make the best salary I could. Jayson and I had both been at high earning periods in our careers. All of that shattered along with everything else.

I've done quite a few things that have given me various skills throughout my life, but one of the things I truly loved was being trained as a coach. I had the good fortune of practicing by coaching executives and emerging leaders within my organizations. I'd also done some individual coaching for clients in my off-hours. I thought, "What if I made that a business? What if I dove into that full time?" The idea had so many attractive aspects to it. It was a career option that I could pursue from home. That would keep me off the roads during the commuting time and give me more time with my children. It was also scalable. I could control my client load to be sure I would be available when my children needed me. If I needed to scale my income up, I could take on more clients. The more I thought about the idea, the more I liked it. My decision was made. I was going to hang out my shingle as a coach.

The field of coaching is a lot like the Wild West. Anyone who has ever advised anyone on anything likes to call themselves a coach, when in reality, coaching isn't advising at all. If you look up "coaches" on any professional directory, you'll be met with a variety of types of coaches offering a variety of outcomes. Executive coaches, personal coaches, life coaches, lifestyle coaches, fitness coaches, parenting coaches, and the list goes on. The training for these coaches is all over the board. Some coaches have spent time in rigorous training studying their craft. Others have sat through a one-hour workshop and are suddenly certified coaches. The field is a buyer beware landscape. Some coaches promise wealth, some promise happiness, and some promise the perfect body. The savvy buyer knows that perfect is not a salable commodity.

Having decided to pursue this career option, my challenge was differentiating myself in a sea of possibilities. My training was of a high caliber. I had completed both a core essentials coaching program and then an advanced coaching program through one of the flagship training schools in the coaching industry. I was a member of the International Coaching Federation and held one of their credentials. My coaching followed their code of ethics and was focused on client outcomes. I felt like I had it all in order —

not to mention the LLC was already in place. I had put it together years ago when I toyed with the idea of becoming a professional coach at that time.

One of the things that most terrified me about this venture was the idea of making a mistake. Since I was a little boy, I never wanted to do anything unless I could do it perfectly. I wanted to be an expert at whatever I tried. I liked the learning and the mistakes to be done in private and not be visible to anyone else. In the months after you lose your spouse, one of the many pieces of unsolicited advice you get is for you not to make rash decisions or significant financial decisions too early as you won't be able to think them through well enough. I have to say that's fair. The first year after Jayson's death was a time of really just trying to hold things together. I had no idea if it was too early to jump into a new career and start a business, but here I was.

Coaches are often encouraged to find their niche. They are encouraged to be highly specific in the areas in which they coach. These niches are typically developed from the broad categories of executive coaching and life coaching. My struggle right out of the box was that I wanted to do holistic coaching. I had this idea, and still do, that executives and leaders in organizations need to bring their whole selves to work. To do that, they have to reconcile who they are as a person with who they are as a leader; none of that fits neatly into a box. So my first published website was filled with some of the most confusing narratives I think I've ever written. I didn't know what to call what I was doing. Consequently, those reading about me had no idea how to classify me, and more importantly they had no idea if they needed anything I was selling.

I had a checklist of the things I needed to be doing. I was going down my list and checking things off as done. The quality of those things was questionable at best. In my mind, I thought I was making a big splash as a coach — a splash that everyone would see and they would know that I was different and that I was exactly what they needed. In reality, that wasn't at all what was happening.

I needed to acknowledge that the emperor was wearing no clothes. I was awkwardly naked in public.

As I began to ask colleagues for feedback and opinions on my marketing materials and website, I wasn't ready for what I received. The feedback wasn't good at all. While I had been doing all the recommended things for a blooming business, I had not done them in a way that would resonate with my target audience. Instead of focusing on the feedback I was getting and going deeper on the points that had been raised, I shopped for even more feedback. When you do that, you're certainly going to find it. I did. What I found were even more opinions on why my materials and website weren't going to work to connect me to clients. Every marketing expert had a thought. The more I sought, the more differing opinions I would get. I drifted further and further away from trying to find what wasn't working at the core of what I had done, and I focused on what someone else would have done in my place. What followed was iteration after iteration of my website, with each iteration being more obscure and esoteric than the last. Ultimately, I drove myself to a place where I wasn't even clear on what I wanted to do.

One of the things I focus intensely on with clients is authenticity. While that is a buzzword that can easily be misinterpreted, I like to work with my clients to reflect and be able to honestly find their authenticity. Why wasn't I doing that for myself? I listened to many people telling me who they thought I was or even who I should be. They were laying their ideas and expectations at my feet and expecting me to pick those up and carry them on my path. It was defeating.

After you lose your spouse, you have to navigate a sea of uncertainty. You're terrified of making the wrong decision. You want someone to tell you how to do it, or you want to find a game plan from someone who has been down this path so that you don't have to figure it out on your own. Every year thousands of grieving individuals spend millions of dollars on grief materials that promise them an easy path to healing. They're lulled into thinking that there is a linear path through grief, and if they can just get to the other side, they'll have a shiny new life. What makes these quick fixes so dangerous is that they are flooded into the market along with sound, therapeutic works by licensed professionals whose job it is to help the grieving heal. There is a marked difference between critical-incident stress debriefing with a licensed professional and someone telling you how to heal because they've been through grief before.

The uncertainty is real and tangible. In areas where we would have been highly decisive, we suddenly find ourselves uncertain and hesitant. We are so terrified of not knowing what the right decision is that we will choose not to make any decision at all. That is where I found myself as I started down the path of this business of coaching. The more I listened to others about what I should be as a coach and how to sell what I do in my practice, I became depressed. I questioned my decision to even go down this career path. Being in this mental state at this point in my grief journey was difficult. The questioning didn't stop with my decisions about my coaching practice but began to permeate all of the other choices I was making in my life, especially as they related to my daughters.

I began to compare myself to other coaches. Comparison is such a dangerous path because we are rarely comparing apples to apples. I would find life coaches enjoying immense success and I would compare myself to them, even though I wasn't doing pure life coaching. I was more experienced — more credentialed. I wasn't having near the success in my practice that they were. I wasn't even doing life coaching. So it wasn't a good comparison at all. My only focus became a focus on what wasn't going well and why it wasn't as good as someone else. It became a darker time in an already dark era. The only feeling I could seem to muster was a feeling of failure.

One of the external factors that negatively influenced my ability to get my practice launched was the onset of the global coronavirus pandemic. The month after I opened for business, the world went into lockdown. Business and the workplace would never be the same. A crucial aspect of pandemics is that we can't control them. I gave myself no grace for this mitigating factor. In my mind, my business should be up and running and generating clients. Never mind that thousands of companies were shuttering. Never mind that millions of people were out of a job. I was in a state where I felt like I should be able to control the success of my business. However, I had a very narrow definition of control and an unrealistic definition of success.

When I work with clients on finding their resilience and embracing their self-acceptance, we do some heavy lifting in the area of mindfulness. We have to realize what we control and what we do not control and know the difference. I had allowed myself to be blinded by a need for control. I could no more prevent the onset of the pandemic than I could control the orbit of the moon. But I somehow felt like I should have.

I remember sitting up late one night. My girls were in bed, and I was listening to music, thinking about what I might do the next day to make my life different. That's when I realized where I was emotionally. I was so far down a path of feeling like a failure and being ready to give up on the business that I had completely lost my ability to be objective and simply accept what was in front of me without judgment. I had allowed myself to be covered up with all of that mess.

A remarkable thing happens when you engage in mindfulness and acceptance. The struggle lessens. When I stopped thinking that these things were happening to me and started thinking more about the simple fact that they were just happening, I could think about strategies to deal with them. That's when I decided to pivot on my company name and move from the self-avowed Jakob Franzen Coaching, LLC to simply The Modern Coaching Company. Why not let the name of my business reflect more about what I wanted to do with coaching? How often did people decide to launch a coaching company in a global pandemic? This was novel, and I needed to react in a novel way.

I think it's important to say that simply changing my company name didn't result in an immediately full book of business. It did result in a change of mindset that helped pull me out of the gloom of thinking my business was failing. It put me into an attitude of giving myself grace and patience. Launching a business amid a global pandemic would take more time. Consequently, it would take more patience and exponentially more grace on my part. A new mindset and a renewed sense of patience put me on a better path, but it's hardly been a perfect one.

One of the hardest things to do has been to play with some of what I'm doing. As we age, we're taught that play is something that we have to put on the shelf and not revisit especially as it relates to work. The truth is that play is essential to us as human adults. The stress and the pressure that is placed on us can cause us to miss those play opportunities. We label them as time-wasters and can even think of them as possibly detrimental to the work that we're trying to do. I specifically avoided play opportunities for the longest time because so much is riding on what I decide to do as my career. After all, there are two little girls for whom I need to provide.

After my mindset shift, the next steps down my path were about finding clarity. At this point in my life, I have learned that any time we decide that we're going to seek clarity, the fog rolls in and roll in it did. However, I had a fresh burst of confidence; I tried to be all things as a coach. I decided I'd be a partner for a popular publisher of a curriculum for developing teams in the workplace. I decided I'd do parent coaching. I decided I'd add life coaching alongside executive coaching. The list of my service offerings grew, and I found myself further and further away from clarity each time it grew. I was trying to find the thing clients would want to buy, instead of refining the messaging about what I did best and doubling down on getting that message into the world.

I have since learned that people need a clear message so that they can easily discern what you do and, more importantly, what you can do for them. Some of these mistakes were expensive ones. Partnerships and certifications don't come cheap. One of the hardest things to do is to admit that you've made a mistake. But, after a lifetime of making them, I think it does get easier. I took a step back and began to think through some of the things that I was offering. Many of them would have to go. I created a single, defining statement for what I do as a coach, and anything that did not fit that statement had to go. I needed to create clarity for myself and for my potential clients.

In the best of times, these setbacks, clarifications, and new definitions are all part and parcel of the entrepreneur's journey. Most businesses don't start as an immediate success. They take time to build, and the path to success is full of missteps, trials, and errors. But in a global pandemic, these missteps seemed to cost me more time. In other businesses I had started, the momentum increased after every retry and every fine-tuning moment. However, as I've worked to get this business off the ground, for some reason I feel like I'm continually screaming into the void. Every business article I read on coaching talks about how it has grown in leaps and bounds during the pandemic and become a multi-billion dollar industry. My efforts have continued to be largely stagnant. Like anything else I do, I've ensured that my education and experience are the best they can be. I'm recognized by my peers and credentialed in the industry. Some of it comes down to the skill of sales and selling, which has always terrified me.

Even as a kid, I can remember being asked to sell things for school or organizations I had joined. I hated it! I hated every minute of it. I sold chocolates no one wanted, overpriced wrapping paper, poorly written greeting cards, and even ubiquitous magazine subscriptions. Sold is probably a bold word. I was a quiet kid who didn't like to impose on anyone. After making my way through family and my parents' friends, I would throw in the towel. As an introvert, I hated talking to strangers, and I certainly didn't want to ask them if they'd like some over-priced chocolates or subscriptions to magazines they wouldn't read. After all, these weren't things that I would have bought myself. Not only did I lack the skill set for sales, but I also didn't believe in the products I was being asked to sell.

Things are a little different now. I believe in coaching. I have a mentor coach and have engaged in coaching for myself whenever I thought it would be beneficial. It has always been helpful. After 30 years in business, I also have decent business acumen. I understand how to set up a business so that the administrative side of it runs smoothly. I have financial software, phone lines, a website, professional email, and portal software. All of these little things make for an excellent experience for my clients. It's easy for them to schedule time with me, and it's easy for me to show up to coach. The problem is, and remains, as it does for many coaches, pulling in new clients.

My social feeds are filled with "coaches who help coaches" get clients. Most of them are thirst traps of guys with abs on beaches in the Caribbean telling me how they can fill my appointment calendar each week with qualified clients for some low, low undisclosed price. They tell me my life can look like theirs. I'm dubious. Despite my respect for the younger generation and their aptitude for digital marketing, at some point, I feel like experience needs to play a role. I also think it's more than simply knowing what to do; it's also knowing how to do it. I've spent hours and hundreds of dollars following marketing formulas for social media ads only to have those ads yield zero clients. As much as I don't like comparing myself to other coaches, I compare what we're messaging and how we're using the platforms. In many cases, even though our core message may be different, we're using the media in the same way. Their engagement is high, and mine is undoubtedly low to none.

It's frustrating. Building a business is never an easy task, but my point here is that trying is what's important. Being resilient doesn't mean that I will jump right in and create a new and successful business. Business success depends on various conditions, and those conditions aren't necessarily easier just because you've decided to go into business after a trauma. Those of us who have experienced loss are told stories all the time about how someone else who had a loss decided to move forward, and then they created a new and wildly successful business. We're led to believe that the act of moving forward was what brought them success. In reality, it was probably a combination of luck, talent, and demand.

The resilience in that story is the act of deciding to take the chance. There is no guarantee that the chances we take will be rewarded with success. Our resilience is moving forward from loss to a place where we can be brave enough to take the chance on keeping our job, finding a new one, or starting a new business venture. For me, it just felt right to start my business. I wanted to do something that I love, something I think I'm good at and something that will allow me to be more involved with my children. Those things are what drew me into starting a business. The initial success with my clients is what has kept me moving forward with it. Like any business, at some point I'll hit the make or break the mark. After all, running a business isn't a hobby for me; it's a way to support my family and provide for my daughters. The particular course I've chosen may not be the right path. If I have to make other choices, that becomes resilience of a different kind. Nevertheless, my resilience after loss is giving this a try and being brave enough to do what I love.

Starting a business isn't for everyone. Resilience after loss can take many forms for some of us. For me, it means starting a business and changing up how I go about making my living. For others, it may mean approaching the job they hold and love in a new and different way. As much as we may want to, we can't always walk away from earning a living after we lose a loved one. I was very tempted to explore ways to retire because I just didn't want to face having to work every day with such a giant hole in my heart. But at my age and with two little girls still to raise, it just wasn't an option. Realizing I still had to take care of things like braces, summer camp, and college tuition meant that I had to get back on track and find the right way to support my family. That is my resilience.

Of course, none of these things is guaranteed. My first year after my loss, I was in a job that wasn't the right fit at all, despite how much I thought it would be. It met many of the criteria I had for taking a job before my world crumbled, but I failed to see how much it wasn't right in the aftermath. You could say that it was a swing and a miss. I'm currently in the middle of my second swing. There are so many aspects of the entrepreneurial path that feel right to me, but again, there are no guarantees. If my current endeavors end up being amiss too, then I'll have to re-evaluate. The point is that the strength and the courage to re-evaluate is the resilience, not the succeeding at any one particular thing.

I still have days when I'm scared. I have two little girls who depend on me for everything. They don't know just how much stress I'm under every day to make some sort of magic happen. When I have those days where I'm scared, I've learned to accept them. They come with the territory. Being scared of having days of uncertainty doesn't mean that I'm not resilient or that my resilience is faltering. It simply means that I'm human. I hope that one day I'll get it all together and be back on track with my career, whether it's this one or something completely different.

As I look around my professional network, I see some colleagues with over 30 years in their current profession. They seem happy and excited about continuing forward with what they do. Others are happily pursuing some new incarnation. They are just as satisfied with what they are now doing. In the months after losing someone, there is nothing wrong with re-evaluating what makes sense for you as a career. After all, we see things from a different perspective, and if we're open, we may even find ourselves on a different path. Resilience is the strength to re-evaluate and to look at things differently.

7

A Virtual Park Bench & Digital Pigeons

In the wake of loss, there is a flurry of attention. People rush to express their sympathy and to offer their condolences. People surround us and what some of us would prefer in those first few days is to be left alone with our grief. We want time to process our feelings privately without prying eyes on us. However, others tend to think that we need not be left alone and so they are constantly there, at least for a while. As the days march forward and they sense that we can function to their satisfaction, they stop coming around. When things calm down and we have to start engaging in making our lives function, this is actually when we need that support the most. As I learned, those were the days when their support would vanish. I realized then just how much I would be on my own as this new life unfolded.

Most humans are social creatures. Even those of us who are introverts tend to work to build community. Our circles are just different sizes. Some of us create vast and elaborate community networks, while others create small and much more intimate groups for support. In either case, these communities that we build are with us as we experience profound events in our lives.

We celebrate with these people when we win or accomplish a long held dream. They are there when life serves up complex challenges and when we are hit with the unexpected. What happens when those communities break down? In the wake of the loss, we can be surprised by the loyalty of friends who settle in, take the place of whole communities, and emotionally support us in the most unexpected ways.

I'm not sure I ever went about community building in the most effective way. I came out late in life. It was a traumatic and challenging time that resulted in collateral emotional damage to others as I sought to live my truth. The more honest I became about who I was with myself, the more the community I had built up in the years before I came out began to wane. My community grew smaller and smaller until it was practically non-existent. The destruction of that network was never intended, but those people knew me as someone else — the man I had pretended to be to hide who I really was. I had decided to be honest about who I was with myself, my family, and those around me. That move was met with varying levels of support. Many, whom I loved, decided they just could not love me because of who I was.

After I came out, I had hoped that I would be met with support from the gay community. I wanted to go out and be among my people. For some reason, I thought deciding to live my truth would be something others would celebrate. Even in my thirties, I could be grossly naive. In actuality, no one cared. I lived in a city of young, openly gay men who looked at me more like a cliché than as a diverse addition to the community. I was just another guy in his thirties who had walked away from a life of pretend.

I eventually did find some support. It wasn't easy, and I wasn't always welcomed in many circles. Despite not ever feeling like I belonged, I began to make some friends who gave me the strength to start to come out at work and begin to live more and more unapologetically as a more authentic version of myself. Interestingly, those friends would nudge me closer and closer to meeting my husband. Neither of us was deeply involved in the gay community, but we became deeply involved with each other through these friends. As a result of this, we still felt some tie to the larger community and wanted to continue to be a part of it.

But, as most things do, things changed as we became more of a couple. There was less going out and more staying in and doing things with other couples. We threw dinner parties, attended barbecues, and did beach vacations with other couples, both gay and straight. We pieced together a rich, diverse, and intimate community of friends. These were the people with whom we celebrated and held onto during the tough times. Looking back, I'm pretty proud of the little community we built.

Again, change is inevitable. Everyone grows, and sometimes that growth means that you grow apart from those you know and love. This growing apart can be natural and is often without any malice. Sometimes we make new friends. Sometimes we move to a new city to chase new dreams. Sometimes we focus on ourselves. That's exactly what we did. Jayson and I decided to have children, which dramatically changed the community's landscape for us. We suddenly found ourselves focused on home life, early morning feedings, and sleep. This was the domain of new parents. Jayson worked 24-hour shifts at the hospital, which added complexity to what we could and could not do.

The obligations of parenthood, with our first child and certainly with our second, began to run counter to the spontaneity of meeting friends for drinks, planning weekend getaways, or even joining friends for dinner. Finding sitters was a tricky proposition, and because of Jayson's schedule, we usually only had one or two weekends a month where we could do anything social. Soon enough, the invitations stopped, and our ability to offer any invitations stopped as well. Our little community became smaller, and life unintentionally became more and more heteronormative. We began to lose our connection to the gay community, and over time it became more and more evident.

After Jayson's death, I thought it might be a good idea, even healthy, to reconnect to the gay community. I felt that reaching out and making more gay friends, and rekindling friendships would be a good idea, especially since Jayson and I had talked often before he got sick about how we needed to revisit those connections. We talked about how we wanted our girls to grow up understanding the battles we had fought to have them. We wanted them to be proud of who we were as their parents and proud of themselves. Social media seemed the right place for an older, chubby guy stuck in the suburbs to make a connection, but I was met with coolness and distance. At the time, I thought it would just take a while. Little did I know that those connections would never rekindle. I was no longer part of that world.

While trying to figure out where I fit and if I had any connection to the community, an old friend emerged. We no longer lived in the same city, but we had kept in touch through the years. He and his partner had come to the memorial service. Our contact had been intermittent at best over the years, but it had been there nonetheless. As I tried to figure things out after the memorial service, I'll never forget what happened one morning while I was sitting on my couch. It was early, and I had made some coffee. I was reading the news and got a notification on my phone. It was him. His message simply said, "Good morning." I remember that my reply was only, "Morning." I couldn't bring myself to say the word good. I had good reasons not to. I had the weight of the world -— my world anyway — on my shoulders. What could be good about any morning?

That exchange started a rhythm of morning conversations where I felt like I could talk about anything with him. It was more needed than I realized. We spoke of things that were deep, heavy, and even heartbreaking. I remember I tried to ask him about his life and challenges because I didn't want it to seem one-sided, but he would always bring the conversation back to me. Every morning with every cup of coffee, there he was. He was checking on me. Making sure I was okay. When I pushed back because I had a hard time accepting help from anyone, his response took me by surprise, and it's one I'll never forget. He simply said, "This is our park bench. We meet here like two old men to have our coffee, start our day with a conversation, and feed the pigeons. Sure, it's virtual, but it's no less our park bench. I'll be here any time you need me."

That made a significant impact on me and still does to this day. He was giving up his time (and often still does) to make sure I was okay. His perspectives helped me see things from a different point of view. He certainly has his struggles and challenges in life, but he set those aside for me in his generosity. At a time when I was struggling to find community and connection, he stepped forward as if to say, "I'll be your community." And he was. He bravely sat on that park bench as I shared everything from my fear to my gut wrenching pain. He would just toss virtual breadcrumbs to digital pigeons and "see" me. He bore witness to the aftermath, which was as expansive as the cataclysm itself. He heard me. My rage, pain, anger, bitterness, confusion, loneliness, emptiness, and longing were all valid in his eyes. "Good morning" became my invitation to show up regardless of how I was feeling. He showed me what it was to consistently bear witness to grief and its aftermath without advising, without qualification, and without judgment.

That time with him gave me quite a bit of strength and perspective. Of course, other dear friends in my life supported me when and as they could. Many of these friends are strong and amazing women, and they have provided invaluable support to me as a father of two daughters. But the park bench conversations were special because they created a space where I could be truly seen as a gay man who had suffered a loss. But what did that mean? I needed to understand better how I might be connected to other men who had experienced a similar loss. As universal as the loss of a partner might be, I needed to know and understand what that looked like for other gay men. My park bench conversations had given me the strength to look, ask, and try to identify with those men.

The first place I thought to look for support was in the online groups through social media. I quickly found a couple of groups that were intended for gay widowers. I joined them both after thinking about it for a couple of days. I'm not sure what I thought I would find in these groups. I was warmly welcomed and found the groups to be generally supportive. I posted my story and received a few comments from others on how sorry they were for my loss. While that was affirming, it didn't create an interpersonal connection. Although I'm certainly not a group meeting type person, I was hoping for more connection — at least a dialogue — in these online groups.

I began to read the posts more and more closely. Men would express their pain, their loneliness, and their anger in those posts. The commenters would range from offering support to being almost rude in telling the poster they needed to move on. I think that's when it struck me that all of us grieve so differently. We can't follow anyone else's recipe for how we're supposed to grieve. The more I read the posts, the more I saw comments that I thought were more hurtful than helpful. Some comments prescribed how long one should wait before emptying the closet. There were comments on when one should start dating again. There were comments on when one should sell the house and start fresh. Grief is complicated, and all I saw was comment after comment seeking to simplify and reduce it to specific advice.

I'm not sure exactly when I decided to leave these groups, but ultimately I decided that the groups were not the place for me. I didn't have the inspiration to offer those grieving. I had grown sad reading so many prescriptive posts about what those who are grieving should be doing. There was a sense that because someone had been through it, they had the answers. Those answers were being rather forcefully given to men who had not asked for them. Ultimately, I left the online social communities. I was disappointed. I wasn't growing, and I wasn't learning anything from the stories I read. I wasn't connecting. Maybe it had something to do with the fact that I had children. I wanted to find more of a connection with men like me. So the next communities I looked at were those belonging to single gay dads.

Being a single dad is an interesting state of being. It has its unique challenges. When I joined the first online group, I was pleased to see that some of the posts were precisely the kinds of thoughts I was having. Some of these men were concerned with making the right choices and the right decisions with their children. Through those posts, I quickly learned how great the variety of single dads is. Some single dads, like me, are created through the loss of their spouses. Some are made because they left a heterosexual marriage to live their truth, and they now co-parent with their ex-spouse. Some are made because they were in a marriage with another man, created a family, and then as some marriages do, theirs came undone. Some single dads are made from the very beginning. Some gay men have chosen to create a family without a partner. These families are built in different ways — from the traditional family to surrogacy, to adoption.

Ultimately, the first group I joined ended up being the best one for me. The other two or three groups I joined were more or less copies of the first. They held the same members or tended toward the same topics. One of them was more about gay dads in general. I had already belonged to a local group for gay dads, and much like that local group, this national group wasn't a good fit for me. While it was nice to see those happy dads and their beautiful families, it made me miss what I had. There was also something off-putting about the highly curated photos that were posted of these families. Every house was immaculate. Every child was perfectly neat. Every dad had six-pack abs. I just couldn't relate. Even when my husband was alive and things were great, they indeed weren't perfect. Our children misbehaved. Our house got messy despite our best efforts. I have never had a six-pack. I didn't stay with the local group or the national group. I barely fit in those groups when my husband was alive and I certainly didn't fit now.

The gay dads' group I chose to stay in suddenly had a post that caught my attention. The pandemic had hit the country with full force. Schools were closed, businesses were closed, and we were all being asked to stay in and not to get out if at all possible. There was so little known about the virus at that point that safeguards were broad and sweeping. It was going to be a hard road, and it hit just as I had decided that it might be healthy for me to meet some new people — especially single gay dads who were dealing with some of the same challenges as I was. Since the world was closed, the virtual landscape of social media was all I, or anyone else for that matter, had. The post appeared as an event coming up on a Sunday in late April. It was going to be a videoconference simply titled "Single Gay Dads Online Get Together."

At this point, I was already an expert with online videoconferences. I managed multiple school meetings each day for my children and for anything I had to do with work. The shy, aloof side of me recoiled from the idea of being on camera with men I'd never met. But the adventurous and curious side of me ultimately won out. What if they could be helpful? What if there was someone nearby I could have coffee with who'd get this crazy new situation? What if I enjoyed myself? I held my breath and marked myself as attending. I made sure the link to the videoconference was in my calendar, and I would be ready. As it turns out, deciding to join that meeting was one of the best decisions I have made.

The group not only met that Sunday but every Sunday and Wednesday after that. As I write this, we're still meeting as the pandemic continues to linger. That first meeting started with the simple premise of, "What will you do if you get sick?" There were so many interesting men on the call with various experiences and various plans; I felt both enlightened and supported as I walked away from that first engagement.

As the group has continued to come together, we have talked through various exciting topics from parenting to sex and dating, mental health and self-care, to vacation plans and dreams after a pandemic lockdown. To say we've grown close is an understatement. We've shared children's birthdays, watched children virtually graduate from high school, and held each other up during some of the hardest of times.

So many of the interactions that have grown between us are precisely the things that sustain some of the best of friendships. It has been both a blessing and a curse to us. It has pulled together some of the best, brightest, and most eligible men from across the country. Some of us could be excellently paired, but we may never know because time and distance are the enemies as the pandemic lifts. Who knows where things will go with the group or how things will end up for any of us? One thing is for sure. We have created a connection that will last long beyond the pandemic or any video conference calls. When the organizer pulled the cork out of that lighting bottle, he made a tribe and I am fortunate to count him as a friend.

Not every community evolves in the same way or is intended to be as intense as the one I discovered with my single gay dad tribe. Some communities serve a particular purpose and are designed to be short-lived. When Jayson died, his work community was already reaching out to support us as a family. His ties to that work community were deep. He had worked with them for years. They had been through quite a bit as a team, and they knew each other deeply. Although they ran the gamut of what could be considered a medical hierarchy, they never seemed to let that dictate how they interacted as people. They each knew their role at work and played it well, but they also respected each other personally and professionally. When one of their own was taken ill, they organized and responded. I was suddenly flooded with calls and with texts. Meals were arranged and delivered. When Jayson died, it didn't stop but intensified.

This group of people, who barely knew me or only knew of me, rallied to my daughters' aid and mine. The meals continued. The texts continued. The calls continued. The visits continued. After the dust settled and I was able to get organized on my own, things began to finally subside. I will never forget those gestures or that group of people. They showed me what humanity was all about. No one ever really asked what I needed. They jumped in and just did what they knew would support anyone in my position. That is kindness and love that will last a lifetime.

Sometimes we belong to communities that we expect certain things from because of their nature. The church is one of those communities. The church my little family belongs to is a small local church. Jayson and I had formally joined but had only been guardedly welcomed. The priest at the time was a kind, young priest who was full of life and good humor. He was, however, clear that we could not be married in the church because he did not want the church to become a lightning rod for what was still a lightning rod issue for the Anglican Communion. While I could understand his position, it chaffed. But we had already been wed in Iowa, where it was legal, by a Unitarian minister we didn't know and in front of a congregation of strangers. Despite his hesitancy, he was interested in us as parishioners and vowed to support us as our minister in whatever way we needed.

That little church served as the place where Jayson and both of our children were baptized. I had long ago been baptized and confirmed in another life. We attended as we could, but as with many new parents, our schedules and energy levels weren't always cooperative. Subsequently, I think we found it challenging to make a complete connection with anyone there. As Jayson grew ill, we were unable to attend, even sporadically, any longer.

When he died, our priest had just moved away. He had gone to a new post, as the clergy do from time to time, in another city and another state. The parish was in the process of finding a new priest, so they were reliant on the vestry and a visiting priest to manage the church. My call was met with confusion and what felt like a bit of a scramble to oblige my request to conduct the memorial service in the funeral home chapel.

I didn't know the priest who stepped forward. He was, of course, kind and gentle. He was a bit older than me and retired. When I arrived at the church to go through the service with him, it was a cold and icy winter day. We sat in his warm office and talked through the options. I told him stories about Jayson to try to give him a background on the parishioner to whom he'd be bidding farewell despite never having met him. We made the necessary adjustments for the service to be a memorial since Jayson had been cremated. I left with my homework to pick readings and music. As I slipped across the ice to get back in my car, I couldn't help but feel a little empty. I was asking someone neither of us had known to perform something that was very intimate. A stranger or not, it's what my husband wanted, and I was not about to break a promise.

The service was tough. I thought I'd be ready for it, but it hit far more brutal than I could have anticipated. We held the service in the large chapel of the funeral home. I was so worried that it would end up being too large because I was unsure how many people would attend. As I sat with my daughters, listened to the music, and watched the slide show, I couldn't hold back the tears. They just kept coming. It was the kind of weeping you want to control, but you simply cannot because it takes over your entire being. At times my entire body shook. People stopped by to offer their condolences. It was all I could do to acknowledge them.

As it got closer and closer to starting time, the pews began to fill. The main section of the chapel was quickly full. The side section filled almost as quickly. Finally, there was only standing room left in this ample space. My husband was loved. Of course, I loved him, but every life he touched resulted in love. I was honored and humbled that so many would come to pay their respects. That love spilled over to me. As the service ended, so many people came to hug me and tell me how sorry they were.

On the counter at home was a beautiful sympathy card. Several had begun arriving, and some came from some unexpected places. There was a card from our physician and his nurse practitioner. The thoughtful and surprising cards tend to take your breath away. The card that caught my eye wasn't from anyone we knew. The card showed up almost right away and was from my mother-in-law's church. They had moved to surround her with support and love, and in doing so they had swept the girls and me into their love as well. I had probably only ever attended her church a handful of times, but I knew she was well respected in her congregation. This card drove that home. Not only did they respect her, but they loved her, and they were acting on that love. The card still sticks out in my memory. It serves as a stark juxtaposition to our church. Our church never sent my daughters and me a card. There was never a call, never a visit, not even a typical southern casserole. Nothing!

I also remember looking for emails and checking for any sort of announcement. The congregation of our church is older. So unfortunately, we lost members regularly. As any parishioner died, their death was announced in a parish-wide email. No email ever came for Jayson. At the time, I was angry. We were never able to attend as much as we had liked, but we had tried to stay connected as much as we could. As our children got older, we had more time to attend until the illness came. Although with time my anger subsided, it gradually turned into disappointment. I had thought our church community would be one of the most supportive communities to which we belonged. It turned out to be one of the least supportive. Given everything that was going on with the transition of clergy and the death of a lesser-known parishioner, I'm confident the absence of the church wasn't on purpose or with malice. But they were, nonetheless, absent. At a time when I felt like my cries to heaven had echoed back to me from an empty sky, the community I thought would hold me up abandoned me instead.

Faith is an interesting concept. At its core, faith is the ability to believe in something or some power that can't be seen. When Jayson was sick, I had so many people telling me to have faith that he would recover. I tried — I really did. I tried to have faith and believed and hoped that he would get better. Instead, with every prayer he took a turn for the worse. I spent a whole year praying and watching him die. But ultimately, what are prayers, if not wishes that we dress up in the pretense of religion and hope some omnipotent power will grant them. In the end, the outcome of prayer is the same as chance.

So, where does this leave someone who grew up in the church with a faith that prayer worked and believed that God was an omnipotent and benevolent being? It leaves me stepping back. I need a break from all of it to reconsider. I need a break to recalibrate how I think about faith, about God, and what it all means. Growing up, I always struggled with God not answering a particular prayer. Some blamed His non-response squarely on me. Somehow, I wasn't good enough, or perhaps I needed to "get my life right," or it just wasn't His will. But yet it always seemed to be God's will for the favorite football team to win.

I'd like to think my husband's life was worth more than a football game. My recent experience is of a God who abandoned me in my darkest hour and has yet to bother to return. It is an experience of a God, if he does exist, who heard my prayers and chose not to answer them, a God who gave two little girls a front-row seat to the death of their Daddy. So, for now, I don't have the time or desire to entertain such a seemingly petulant and demanding deity.

When you think about it, where I am is a tough spot in which to be. So much of what I believe in about community has been tested or redefined. I've learned so much about how people connect, and specifically how I connect with them, I've also discovered where I don't connect or what happens when community disappoints. That last lesson has been particularly long in coming. A component of self-care is drawing boundaries with people or communities who aren't good for us.

I have tried to fit into groups or communities where I just wasn't welcomed for much of my life. That effort, over time, was damaging. For the entire length of my relationship, I never really had to worry about community or whether or not any particular group would accept me. I was always welcomed at home. Not being accepted can lead to sadness and melancholy. It smarted when I didn't fit in anymore to some of these places, especially after 16 years of belonging at home.

I still think it's essential to build community after you lose someone, even if you're highly independent and self-sufficient. As much as I am perfectly designed to be alone, a part of me still longs for connection and longs to be part of something bigger than myself. Some of us keep that desire pushed far down in our psyche, while others engage it often. What is important to remember is that grief irrevocably changes you. The way you used to fit, even in the communities that are the most familiar to you, will have changed. Rebuilding takes an awful lot of being open and allowing. It takes vulnerability.

All of that comes into play when we're ready. I learned that every community to which I want to belong might not yet be prepared for me. That's okay. My awareness of how I fit and how I grow with others is far more critical than the number of communities that accept me. For now, I know I'm always welcomed on my virtual park bench feeding digital pigeons. That fuels my resilience.

8

Dating Men & Finding New Happiness

It was another one of those talks. We'd had far too many of them in the last few weeks. I didn't like talking about what life would look like without him. Even though we still thought we'd have more time, or at least I did, he wanted to discuss how I would face the future without him. I think it may have been his way of wanting to help, to offer his advice, or maybe even a way for him to feel like he had at least a little bit of control over what was coming. This particular evening's conversation was centered on me finding happiness after he was gone. That subject matter made it even more uncomfortable for me.

I was folding laundry. That was usually his job because he preferred his folding methods to mine. Something about the way that I folded things just wasn't quite right for him despite my efforts at symmetry and wrinkle-free creases. He enjoyed doing it because he would watch some sort of science show on TV and fold away. I'd usually help put things away. But now, his energy was waning, and folding laundry had become a task that took too much energy for him to do. I happily took it up, and I could tell he was grateful. He never once criticized a fold or how anything was put away. That evening, the stacks of clothes were finished on the bed, our daughters were watching some TV after dinner, and the house was relatively quiet.

"You know, after you grieve me for a respectable amount of time, you really should put yourself back out there," he said. I tried not to make eye contact as I carried clothes through the bathroom to the closet. He had seated himself on the side of the tub to be able to see me whether I was in the closet or the bedroom. I had to pass by him with each trip to the closet.

Always trying to deflect with humor, I replied, "And how long is respectable?"

"No less than six months, but no more than about 12," he said quickly.

His answer was oddly specific. He had thought about this. I had no idea how long I would grieve, and I certainly didn't want to think about doing it. As I walked back through the bathroom, I could tell by the look on his face that he wasn't finished. He had more to say. If there was anything I had learned from him in 16 years of being together, it was that he was going to finish saying what was on his mind. I had no chance of ending this conversation any sooner. It was charming that the thought of my happiness was on his mind, but I wasn't sure we needed to be talking about it. He continued.

"Promise me that you'll put yourself out there at least after about a year."

"I'll think about it. I'm sure I'll need to focus on parenting and will have my hands full with all of that."

"I know how you are," he said. "You'll cut yourself off and do things for everyone except yourself. Just promise me.

How can you not make that promise? He wanted some reassurance in his decline that I would pursue happiness after he was gone. Didn't he realize how much happiness I had been given with him?

I wanted to tell him how much that was enough and that I didn't need to go looking for anything else. I tried to tell him that I needed to devote myself to our daughters to ensure they would get off to a great start in life. I wanted to say to him that I had never loved anyone like I loved him and probably wouldn't ever love anyone else like that. I didn't. That's not what he needed to hear from me. He needed to hear that I would be okay. He needed reassurance.

"Fine," I said. "I'll put myself out there."

"Great. I want you to find happiness."

"Well, whomever I find certainly won't be you." I quipped.

"Of course not!" He laughed. "But you deserve to be happy. And if you can't find a good man to date, at least have sex with twenty-somethings." At this point, he laughed so hard he was coughing. He had absolutely cracked himself up. Just because he thought I was handsome, he assumed everyone else would too. I laughed because I'm not sure anyone had given me a second look in years. I didn't even want to think about what dating would look like in my fifties.

A year passed quickly after he died. It was a challenging year. I was dealing with the stress of a job that wasn't right for me. I was trying to maintain some normalcy in my daughters' lives and bracing myself for what was unfolding as a global pandemic. In the quiet before bed one night, I remembered his words. "Promise me." Anyone who knows me knows that I always keep my promises. I get incredible amounts of anxiety if I am unable to or even think I may be precluded from keeping a promise. I sat in bed one night, unable to concentrate on the program I was watching. I needed to keep the promise I had made him. I wondered how I would even put myself out there. After all, the only gay person I routinely spoke with lived three hours away and had a partner. It wasn't like I was part of the scene anymore, and there wasn't a regular group on whom I could depend for introductions. I couldn't think of a single gay man at all.

Jayson and I had initially met as a result of a dating app. Although technically it wasn't an "app" at the time, it was a website. And to be even more technical, it was more because mutual friends nudged us together. We had both been far too narrow in our search parameters, which resulted in us screening each other out because of height. My falling for him had much less to do with his online profile and more to do with how he captured my heart the night we met. It seemed like it was so long ago, but I remembered every detail. We grew so much in the 16 years together after we met. There were undoubtedly challenges and hardships, but we came through each one stronger and more connected than ever.

Could that work again? I wasn't sure, but I promised him I would give it a try. I navigated to the website I had used so long ago when I met him. It was still a thriving site promising love and connection to singles around the world. There was a slight twinge of excitement as I created a login for the site. Of course, it didn't take long for that excitement to give way to anxiety. The site asked that I upload a set of pictures for my profile. I felt defeated. I had gained so much weight since Jayson's death. The stress of trying to live this life on my own and raise two daughters was overwhelming. I didn't always manage that part well. Fortunately, I had a few pictures I could use that were current and somewhat decent. I wanted to be sure there was some truth in my advertising. I would hate to get someone's attention, only to disappoint them if we met.

I also decided to be truthful in the bio. I led with the fact that I was a widowed dad with two young children. That felt like a significant fact that someone should know right up front. Not every gay man wants to jump into an instant family. I must have re-read the text 20 times. I checked my grammar and the readability over and over to make sure it flowed well but still sounded casual. No one needed to know how stressed this whole business made me. Finally, after double-checking and making sure I'd filled in all the blanks, I posted my profile. Then it came time to pay. Online dating had gotten quite a bit more expensive than I remembered. I reviewed the options and decided to go with a three-month subscription. Surely that would give me enough time to know whether or not this would work for me. I entered my credit card number, and it was done.

As any of us who have done online dating know, there are a variety of filters and search criteria that you can use to screen out and screen in potential matches. As I began to browse the profiles in my locale, I noticed their ages. These men were mostly in their thirties. They looked young, vibrant, and many of them were ready for their first serious relationship. I had been in that age group the first time I had joined the site. Like them, I had the world by the tail, and anything was possible. As I scrolled through their smiling faces, it suddenly began to dawn on me how significant the age difference was. I had indeed lived an entire lifetime in those years between our ages. How different I must be to them. I'd experienced so much life. I'd traveled, bought property, been on the forefront of gay marriage, experienced surrogacy twice, and been widowed. So much of life was still new to them. I couldn't possibly be a match. I adjusted the criteria to men closer to my age.

The number of possible matches dropped significantly. Many men my age no longer needed to find a match. Most of them were still with the men they'd met in their thirties. The profiles moved into the more awkward variety with this set. Some men were frustrated by the dating scene. Their bios were sarcastic and biting. They had had enough games that so often get played in dating that they screened the players out upfront. Then there were the men who'd enjoyed their singleness for longer than they had intended. They were ready to settle down, but they weren't sure how to do that from their very social lives based on their profiles.

I thought about my own life. At this age, I had reached a point where I knew what I liked and how I liked it. I kept my home a certain way. There were certain brands I enjoyed. There were specific and proper ways to do things. I had made my peace with avoiding crowds and traveling in a higher fare class. It gave me pause to think of doing something with someone else who had other ideas about how life should be. I had been with someone for 16 years who challenged me and grew with me in the same directions. To have a successful relationship, I'd have to let some of that go. I wasn't sure that I could do that.

It didn't take long to get through the profiles that were on the site. I felt a little let down by the whole process. I thought there would be more. I thought my profile might get a little attention. After all, the picture I had managed to find was flattering. However, there wasn't a single notification. Everyone I'd ever talked to about dating had always talked about being on the apps. In other words, they talked about being in more than one. Indeed there was more to this online dating thing. I explored and looked at some other recommended dating apps. There were apps for any level of commitment you wanted to make, from serious to casual, and apps for any taste of sexual encounter. I found another reputable app for more serious dating. I downloaded the app to my device and started building a new profile.

Luckily, I cut and pasted much of my bio from the other site I had started with. I uploaded my pictures and was ready to go with this new app in half the time. But as soon as I made my profile live, it was time to pay. This was going to get expensive. I chose another three-month plan and began trying to get the hang of the app. The basis of this app was swiping left or right on the picture to indicate interest. I tried to read the bios that looked interesting to me, but most men were not filling in their bio at all. This got frustrating for me quickly. Sure, I could decide in a glance if a man was good looking, but what kind of substance was there to him? That was as important to me. As much as I'd like to say it's the most important, that would be a lie. Attraction, for me, is a whole package kind of deal. I have to be physically attracted, but beyond that I am certainly drawn to substance and intelligence, not to mention decisiveness and a wicked sense of humor.

I'd love to say that is where the story ends. That I found some amazing man in those three months and we are now living happily ever after. However, that is far from what happened. There was lots of swiping and scrolling and scrolling and swiping. Some profiles repeated themselves after a while. I found that I often accidentally "liked" a profile by clicking the wrong button or swiping in the wrong direction. Sometimes, those connections would end up in conversation. Usually, those conversations would die out after time. At the end of three months, I began to realize that putting myself out there also meant keeping myself out there. I'd have to subscribe for longer. I decided to take a little break from being out there and waited to subscribe again.

After a taking a break, putting myself out there again resulted in actually meeting some of these men. I would soon learn that is no easy feat for a single parent. To meet someone and spend any appreciable time with them at dinner required a sitter. For me, sitters have never been easy to find. The few that I had in my contact list were highly qualified and well-referred, which of course, meant that they were also in high demand. So that meant that I had to plan far ahead to do anything. There were no spontaneous meetings. I would also soon learn that this was frustrating to the men who wanted to meet me, but didn't completely understand what it meant to have to juggle children. Sometimes, everything would fall through, and I'd be wished good luck by an otherwise nice man who just didn't have the patience to wait around.

I do get it. If you're not used to children and all of the obligations that come with parenting, I'm sure it's frustrating. The more I had exposure to men my age, the more I realized that they were either retiring or getting ready to retire. Their lives were much more focused on leisure time, and they spontaneously scheduled things on a whim. My life was dedicated to parenting and to providing. I was juggling being an entrepreneur with trying to provide my children with the most normal life possible. I'm not sure any of them were ready for just how significant a role either of those things played in my life.

Men who were on the younger end of the spectrum would like the idea of dating someone who had children, but they weren't quite ready for the reality of what that meant. The idea that I needed to be home by 11:00 p.m. to relieve the sitter was foreign to them, primarily if they were used to enjoying a late-night when going out. Their lives centered around work, the gym, and social events during the week. The idea that it could take up to two weeks for me to schedule a date with them was just too daunting. All of this got more complicated with my desire to keep my children from meeting anyone until I was sure that they'd be around a while. My children didn't need a parade of strangers coming in and out of our lives. Since there was only ever a handful of first dates, that was never an issue.

I can still count the dates I had on one hand. I wish I could point to a specific reason why none of them worked out, but in all honesty there are layers of reasons. There is an awkwardness to dating after having had a long and successful relationship. It's hard to let things just unfold in the now and appreciate the newness of meeting someone when what you miss is the deep, emotional intimacy of what you had. That intimacy developed over time in the previous relationship, and it would have to develop over time in any new relationship. It can't be rushed Meanwhile, there's a lot of holding back and mental speculation occupying one's thoughts.

None of these dates felt quite right. No matter how I played things out in my head, I just couldn't make myself be a good fit for any of them. There was also the challenge of energy. By the time I had made it out to dinner, I would have bathed children, cooked their dinner, coordinated the sitter, made sure I had cash to pay her, and the whole evening I would be keeping an eye on the time so that I wouldn't be late to relieve her. None of this felt sustainable. In one of the more recent dates I had, the conversation turned to the question of, "How do you see this working?" I think it was then that it hit me. It wouldn't. There was no way I could keep this up. Just a single dinner took a considerable toll on me both in energy and in money.

When talking about dating with a friend, she said, "I don't think you're ready." The more I thought about what she said, the more I realized that she was right. I put myself out there because I promised my husband that I would. I was so eager to keep my promise to him that I didn't think through whether or not I was ready to keep it. So much about my life isn't fair to someone willing to date seriously. I can't be as available as they may want or need me to be. My life has other immovable priorities. I also did some thinking about what it would look like to combine my life with someone else. That little exercise was terrifying. Despite the trauma and upheaval of loss, I'm pretty settled at this point in my life. I like where I live, my house, and how my girls and I fit together. How could I possibly add someone to that mix?

I remember when Jayson and I combined our lives. Some might say we were pretty settled when that happened. But neither of us had children at that point, and we only had his cat to worry about. We kept the nicest of things that were duplicates and set up an extraordinary life together. Now things have memories attached to them. I have become sentimental in my older age.

We're constantly bombarded with images of shiny happy couples who have survived loss, divorce, or some other tragedy. It makes for an incredible fairy tale to be able to say, "I lost the love of my life, but I have found love again" There are countless video talks, books by widows, and even social media posts about the joy someone has found with a new mate. There is certainly nothing wrong with any of them finding love again. The problem comes up when it's held out as a definition of resilience. To be considered resilient, we don't have to find those things again, and certainly not right away. That process could take years for some of us, and for others, it could be mere months. The timeline is different for all of us, if that is something we choose to do. I'm still not sure it's something I desire. None of it felt right at all, and my mental health improved significantly when I took a step back and simply accepted that it was not going to be a part of my life right now. I deleted and walked away from the dating apps. There is a lightness that takes over when you let go of what you think you *should* be doing.

My friend was right. I wasn't at all ready to date. I'm still not. I'm not sure I ever will be. I'm not sure how Jayson would feel about that fact 36 months after his death, but there it is. One of the things I have my clients work on all the time is acceptance. I'm a firm believer that we have to accept certain things as they are, without qualification or judgment. This way we can make better decisions as it relates to those things. To do that, we have to let go of so much of the emotion that traps us. Not everything needs our emotional response. For me, this is one of those things. I'm learning that dating, romance, sex, and love just aren't part of my life right now and they probably won't be in the near term. Maybe not even in the far term. I'm withholding judgment on those things. The idea that I am enough is slowly permeating all of the different areas of my life.

I've always been focused on the future. My life has been about preparing or getting ready for some future event or life era. It feels good to focus on the here and the now. I simply need to be enough, and that means that I don't need a connection with someone else. I don't need to worry about what the future will look like for me. Being able to be present and not get caught up in the past or the future is definitely resilience.

Who knows what Jayson would have done with the time I have left if he were in my shoes, but the point is, it's my time, and what I do with it may be entirely different from what he would do or would want me to do. After all, I'm becoming another person in his absence. However, I have to reconcile the promise I made to him with how I choose to live my life. At this point, I can honestly say that I put myself out there. It's done. I made the effort. I think in his mind, he thought that finding love again would be easy and that it would bring me happiness. He always was concerned for my happiness and the fact that he was still thinking about it, even when he was sick, is a testament to the kind of man he was. I never had to doubt just how much he cared about me or just how much he loved me. But maybe my happiness is down a different path than that of having a relationship again. I'm finding that happiness in this new life is relative.

There is a certain beauty to solitude. My daughters make sure that I'm never really alone, but it's beautiful in those times that I am. I have time to think and time to just be. We often focus too much on making ourselves a part of a couple and want so much to be in a relationship that we forget the beauty of being alone with ourselves. I'm not one who is given to loneliness. Being alone is one of those conditions that I can genuinely accept at face value without qualification or judgment and simply enjoy the solitude.

As I think of the future, I don't think of it as being with someone else. I think about everything I will get to do with my daughters as they mature into young women. While life is comfortable for us now, I don't know where we'll be in six months or even a year. I will always be looking out for the best path for them, for the course that helps them achieve their dreams and sets them up for success. My goal is to help them flourish in life. Even after I've had the good fortune to see them off to college, my thoughts turn to a downsized place in a quiet little town and a life of utter simplicity. One of my favorite writers has always been Henry David Thoreau. He often wrote so eloquently of solitude and his love of it. When reading _Walden_, I found myself envious of his time alone and the simplicity of his life. It is a far cry from my very modern and chaotic life.

So, with those thoughts of simplicity and solitude in my head, I have to say that I don't think dating will be for me and certainly not now. It was an interesting experiment and one I think many of us try after losing a spouse. It's funny, the other part of that promise to Jayson, even though he was joking, was to have a good time and enjoy some casual, physical fun even if I couldn't find the proper long-term connection. There are certainly plenty of apps out there for the casual sexual encounter. I'm too terrified of the body-shaming I'd have to guard against. I know my flaws, and I don't need those pointed out to me as a justification as to why I'm not good enough. Ultimately, all of that takes too much energy and is not something I need. It is a complication in an already over-complicated life.

Resilience for me, at least as far as relationships go, is getting back to simplicity. The handful of friends I have are loyal and highly supportive. I'm not sure I need anything more than that. Life is different now, and I want and need other things. Romance just isn't one of those things. Maybe I can mark the promise kept as I did put myself out there, and I did consider having a little fun. But as I become this different person, I realize I don't need either of those things. Life is an adventure, and it's my adventure to have. I can't get caught up in the fact that having a new partner would be some sort of measure of resilience or even success on my part. The resilience is that I'm in a place of choice for all of it, and I choose to go on it on my own.

9

I Belong to Me

Humans seek a sense of belonging. It's how we're made. While it may seem nice to have, all of the evidence points to the fact we're healthier for a sense of belonging. Belonging brings us a sense of acceptance, safety, and support. Clubs, groups, churches, and communities create spaces for belonging for humans with similar interests and shared goals. We choose our universities, careers, social clubs, and even our neighborhoods to increase this sense of belonging. But sometimes, that sense of belonging can get distorted, and we can have trouble fitting in or finding our tribe. When we have to hide part of who we are or pretend to be someone else, we may find that we don't fit in anywhere.

Growing up, I tended to keep to myself. That's not to say I didn't have friends. I did. I grew up in a small town where everyone knew each other and often knew far more about each other than was healthy. Such is rural life. Small towns have a strange sense of community that can very much resemble a family. There is bickering, judgment, and competition until an outsider disparages any member of the community. Then the community closes ranks and protects its own. No matter what any of us thought of each other when I was growing up, we were part of the same community, and for the most part we'd always stand with each other when we needed it.

Some of my earliest memories of school are of standing on the sidelines and watching. I never really felt like I fit with the other kids in my class. Their approach to life was just different. I was reflective and philosophical and engaged in much more risk analysis than my peers.

My parents have often told me about the time when my teacher sent a note home because she was concerned about me. I would stand on the edge of the playground just watching the others play. When my parents asked me about it, I simply replied that I didn't think the other kids were very smart. There was some truth to that statement. The big club at the time required one to eat the leaf of a Chinaberry tree to become a member. I'm not sure how I knew at such a young age, but I was probably told that those trees were poison. I was not about to eat that leaf to belong.

During my entire school career, I tended to drift in and out of belonging. When my talents or skills suited my peers, I was always much more included. I was elected to leadership roles for my class in high school. I started for the varsity football team. But there were always shared secrets and inside jokes of which I was never a part. It certainly wasn't for lack of trying. Just like any other kid, I took some risks to try to fit in, but I never really did. I ultimately found a niche that gave me some sense of being part of my classmates. The problem was that I was running away from who I was.

I had known from an early age that I found men attractive. For a small-town boy, there is no revelation more terrifying. Gay men were often the butt of jokes with my high school friends. This behavior was encouraged and modeled by many of my sports coaches. The message was clear. Gay men were inferior, broken, and would never be as good as "normal men." I had to swallow all of that and tamp it down. I could never let them know who I was, and I worked hard not to have to admit it to myself. Because of that I never really fit in, and I could never really be close to any of my friends for fear that they might find out. I would be horrified if it were ever to be called into question. In my mind, it was far better to live on the edge than to be cast out entirely.

The church's message to me was also clear. I was an abomination. That was an onerous burden to bear because my family was active in our church and strived to be respected in the community. But deep down I knew I didn't belong and that no matter what I did, I'd never be good enough because of who I was. One of the most scarring memories I have is of a hayseed preacher who, when visiting our church, laid hands on me to cast out "the demon of homosexuality". He said it loudly and in front of my friends. He said it in front of my family. All I could do was deny it, and I ended up doubling down on hiding who I was and lived for a while with the terror that I may be possessed. That experience triggered a protracted sense of self-loathing that began to form the basis of how I thought of myself and solidified the feeling I had of never belonging. The quest for belonging became both consuming and elusive.

As I grew older, I tried to find different ways to belong to groups that helped me hide who I was. I enjoyed theater and decided to choose that as my first college major. Even at the conservative university I attended, gay people surrounded me in the theater department. So many people told me that I'd need to be careful so that the gay people didn't suck me in. So I worked very hard not to be or even appear to be a gay theater major. Again, I stood on the periphery because I wasn't true to who I was and never really belonged. I could see a life that would fit me, but I couldn't be part of it. I convinced myself that I didn't belong. I changed my major later that first year to something more mainstream and acceptable. I was embarrassed by who I was and the things I loved.

When we feel like we belong to a group, we like to show people that we have a tribe and we do this by using symbols that we identify ourselves with to convey that sense of belonging. In my search for validation and belonging, I needed my symbol to show that I had moved into a more "respectable" study path. For whatever reason,

I was fixated on owning an HP 12C calculator. I felt like that symbol would show that I was serious about my business study and that I was part of that world. I saved up my money and was finally able to purchase one at the school bookstore. I spent hours learning how to use it and to program it. I was sure to have it out in the library so that people could see that I was doing "serious" work and not simply reading literature or learning lines for a play. Though, I missed doing those things. I had created a false sense of belonging for myself.

In that false sense of belonging, I pushed forward to be a part of the mainstream. I pledged a social fraternity that felt like it could be a good fit for me. It was outside the Greek system but it still participated in mixers and date parties. It would add to the persona I was creating. It would help to show that I belonged. I threw myself into it wholeheartedly. I made some terrific friends, but as I got close to them the alarm bells would go off. Too close, and they might see that I was a fraud — a fraud hiding a secret. How horrified would they be to know that I was gay? How horrified would I be to have to admit it? I met some good men who were strong friends during my college years. But as the groups' adherence to religious dogma increased, I felt more and more disenfranchised. When I came out later in life, most of those friends fell away. I miss them sometimes. However, I had created those friendships under pretense; so I never really belonged.

In those college years and the few years that followed, I worked hard to belong and be a part of all the expectations of me. I joined faith communities that were large and important. I attended bible studies at churches that required police offers to direct traffic on Sundays because of their large congregations. I was sure to attend on Sundays and to be at all of the young, single socials. I wanted so badly to belong. The truth is I didn't and never would. I could never be accepted for who I was. My authentic self was hidden, restrained in a closet with barricades of my own making. Looking back, that was a miserable time in my life. Everything I did created more self-loathing and made me feel like I was broken. I was becoming more and more critical of myself because I wasn't living my truth. I was building a spectacular lie.

Coming out wasn't easy and is certainly a story in and of itself. I came out later in life and I left much collateral damage in my wake as I struggled to get to my truth. I'll never forget my first night out on the town after coming out. I was excited to "be with my people." There was a certain allure to gay life in Austin, Texas. It was visible and arguably accepted in the heart of a very conservative state. I got dressed and headed out to a club by myself. I wasn't sneaking; I wasn't going in secret. I was doing my best to be proud and ready to be accepted by my tribe. Not a single person said a word to me the whole evening. I was met with a collective stare and a yawn or two. I had not made a splash on the scene. There was undoubtedly no tribal initiation. My sense of belonging was bruised.

I shied away from going out again and began to explore other ways to connect with a community to which I was sure I felt I belonged. The internet was still relatively new for me and only accessible with a dial-up modem. My technical side soon found and set up various chat platforms that connected people of varying interests. I found I was less shy in chat rooms and soon made friends in multiple locations, including Austin. It was shortly after that I was pulled into the Thursday night coffee meetings downtown. Gay men would gather to meet and talk IRL (in real life.) It was always fascinating to learn someone's handle and put a face with a name. The young, attractive men in the group soon gained large followings that translated to quite a bit of attention online as well as offline. I made some friends but continued to be on the outside of the community. Even then, as I got closer to some of the men I met, I wasn't indeed myself. I felt the connections weren't as solid as they should have been.

I take responsibility for that. I was jumping in, trying to make connections with other men without really knowing myself. It doesn't take long for the cracks to show when you're unfamiliar with yourself, your wants and desires, and your boundaries.

A lack of connection breeds loneliness. Although I was accustomed to being on my own, I found myself being lonely. Even in the din of Thursday night coffee or time at the clubs afterward, I was lonely in the middle of crowds of people. It was isolating. I tried to date, but I didn't know with whom I would fit because I didn't know myself. Men who attempted to connect with me soon found that getting to know me was like walking on quicksand. I can only imagine how off-putting I was.

It was then that I began to pull away from all of the noise and activity. I had made some close friends, and they were enough. I realized that I needed to learn to belong to myself and understand who I was and what I wanted in life. I needed to be okay with myself. After years of other people not being okay with me and telling me how I wasn't okay, I needed to be okay. I needed not to be embarrassed and hide. I needed to find my pride in who I was.

After spending some time with myself, I decided I would give up on the idea of dating and simply be content with where I was in life. That's when a friend pushed an online dating profile my way. It was one I had not seen because it had been filtered out in my search criteria. This guy missed my height requirement by a couple of inches. I decided what the heck. I messaged him and had no idea that I was about to find out what it was like to continually be challenged to be myself and find a sense of belonging with another human being.

A sense of belonging happens when we feel seen, accepted, and included in a group or something greater than ourselves. While getting ourselves and learning to love who we are is a sense of belonging, we continually seek to be part of something larger. Interestingly, I discovered that more significant could sometimes simply be a group of two. I loved who I was with Jayson. From the very beginning, he accepted me as-is. Of course, I tried to put on a few airs when we first met. I think we all do that to some extent in a new relationship, but he saw right through them and called me out on them. He liked the real me and didn't need to be bothered with anything else. I'm not sure I'd ever felt so accepted by anyone. There were indeed things about me that annoyed him. Humans tend to be annoying. But overall, we both liked who we were, and we liked who we were becoming together.

I'm not sure I realized it at the time, but I've thought about it since he died. I was always in a hurry to get home. I found that I would much rather be home with him than anywhere else. I couldn't wait to tell him about my day, to laugh with him, and to talk about our hopes and dreams for the future. Even when I'd had a bad day, it didn't take very long for him to help me let go of that and to embrace a laugh or two. The more I was with him, the more I got to know myself and see myself through his eyes. After a lifetime of feeling less than and inadequate, suddenly I was enough. I was enough for him, and I was enough for myself. There is a lightness that comes when you're able to let go of self-loathing. It makes room for joy.

The joy is what stands out the most for me. Our relationship certainly wasn't perfect, but it generated so much joy. Our connection was built on honesty, trust, and vulnerability. We knew everything about each other and accepted it all at face value. Our growth was not only together but intertwined in a life of self-discovery and acceptance. I belonged to him, and he belonged to me, and together we were something far more significant than either of us would have been on our own. It is a feeling, a sense of self, which I will never forget.

What happens when you lose that? That is the question that I have wrestled with often since his death. The idea of belonging was essential to us in the years before he died. We had created a fantastic identity as a couple; we'd added two beautiful children and made a family. In each iteration, our belonging was evident. As our lives stabilized a bit more once our children grew out of the diapers stage, we began thinking about how we fit into our world and our community.

At the time, there was still so much negativity around gay marriage and gay people in general. The nation's politics had become toxic, and our community was often a target of the culture wars. We were constantly fighting against misconceptions and preconceptions about a two-dad family. Forms for our children were unfriendly and presumed a husband and wife. When I would be out with our children, I'd get comments like, "Oh, is mommy taking the day off?" I would even get people who would say, "Did mommy fix your hair before she let Daddy babysit?" The truth was I did their hair, and the idea I would babysit my own children was preposterous. From the woman who stalked me in a big box store to the random shopper in a warehouse store, we were constantly being held up to a stereotype and then looked at suspiciously when we didn't measure up to it.

We had lots of conversations about how to work against these assumptions. We talked about how we wanted our daughters to understand how hard we had fought to be married and how hard we had fought to be a family. We wanted them to be proud of who they were and from where they came. So often, they had been placed in the awkward position to make something for one of us on Mother's Day at school. Whenever we were faced with these awkward situations, we had to prepare them to say they would make something for a grandmother, an aunt, or their godmother. They were proud that they had two dads, and we wanted them to continue to be proud. Through various decisions, we had ended up in a house in the suburbs. We were fully participating in that life by raising our children, going to birthday parties with them, and making our commutes to work. In pursuing the life that we thought was best for our children, we also found ourselves completely disconnected from the gay community. We were more or less disconnected from any gay people — period.

While our girls knew they were part of a two-dad family, they also thought they were a bit magical because they didn't know anyone else who had two dads. There were no other gay families that we knew of in our neighborhood. Most of their friends came from two-parent heterosexual families. These parents were undoubtedly good people, and we were able to share experiences with them because of our children, but we still wanted to do more with families that looked like ours. Of course, that is easier said than done. We were part of a gay dads' group and had been for a while but had never really been able to do anything with them. The adult events required that we have a sitter, and those were hard to come by. It also meant paying for extra time since we lived outside of the city and most of the events took place in the city. Family events focused on the children, but more often than not those would fall on weekends when Jayson had to work a 24-hour shift. It was frustrating constantly having to pass up the invitations. Then Jayson got sick and we had to let it all go.

Reconnecting with the gay community was essential to Jayson, but I was unsure about it all. I had never really been connected. He often talked about going to the Pride festivities and bringing the girls so they would have an appreciation for gay culture. I certainly wasn't opposed to that, but I had never been to Pride festivities myself. I felt a little inadequate because I wasn't sure how I was going to help them understand our culture when I didn't understand it fully myself. I had spent our entire relationship secure in the little cocoon of our family. I hadn't given any thought to the community with which I had developed such an awkward relationship when I came out. But at the time, I was game. I'd go down any path with him. He had never let me down, and everything was an adventure.

Now that he's gone, I'm not sure what to do with the adventure. As the girls shared with folks that they lost their Daddy, I still got asked the question of, "Where's mommy?" or "Are you the grandpa?" Strangers are ever questioning my identity as their father. They still know and understand that they came from a two-dad family, but they still don't see any other families like ours. The other day they came home from school so excited to learn that one of their female teachers had a wife and a baby. They felt a bit of a connection between our family and theirs. I was relieved I have continued to teach them that love is love. They clearly understand that, but they associate that with us more generally rather than specifically. After all, a family with only one dad doesn't stand out as a gay family as quickly.

I thought for a long time about picking up where Jayson and I had left off and becoming a part of the community. I wasn't really sure where to start and I couldn't figure out how. After all, shouldn't figuring out how to join in be easy enough at my age? I was frustrated and tired of trying when I finally realized that I had been an outsider since the moment I had come out. After 16 sweet years of belonging, I now found myself right back where I started. I'm not a part of that community, and I don't think I ever will be. Why knock on a door where you're not welcomed? Belonging is such a key component of being human, and belonging to myself satisfies that part of my humanity. I'm enough. In this last chapter of my life, the work before me is accepting that this chapter is about a return to solitude and simplicity. That's my baseline.

I felt lost and adrift after I lost my husband. I would think I'm not the only one who has felt this way. No one ever seems to talk about belonging as it relates to those of us who are widowed. Everyone likes to think that some support system swoops in to take care of those of us who have lost our spouses. In reality, the support system gets fainter and fainter as time goes by. People assume that you're getting stronger and that you're able to live without help or support. They don't realize that you also need a sense of belonging. They forget you might not only need to be invited to things, but you may also need to be politely pushed into them. As much as we all desire to belong to something, it helps when others want us to belong too. I heard someone say once about someone who was grieving, "If she wants to join us, she'll reach out. I don't want to impose." I remember thinking to myself, what if she not only wants you to impose but also needs you to impose. The interesting thing about being lonely and isolated is that you start to think your presence isn't wanted or desired and that nobody truly cares about your existence. I believe it is essential that we reach out, and not just once or twice. We need to send a consistent message to the grieving that they are welcomed and wanted in our groups and as part of our circles.

It's crucial that we give them the emotional support they need to help them stay afloat so that they don't fall into a deep dark hole of depression. Their stories matter and when we take the time listen and allow them to share their stories, like I have with mine, we open the door for healing to occur. When we share our own stories, we're not only healing ourselves but we're also helping others heal along the way. It's a way of letting them know they're not alone — a way of touching someone's heart, a reminder that we're human and the importance of staying in touch with our sense of self.

Being told that they're wanted or they are a needed part of a whole also helps with their reconnection to themselves. I talk all the time about belonging to yourself, and I firmly believe that it's important. We have to be able to see our value so that we can show that value to others. Sometimes we need a little nudge. We need to be reminded that parts of us are truly loved and desired by others. Often we become a better version of ourselves when we're with the right person. After we lose them, we have to learn to become a new version of ourselves without them. Empathy for the widowed can be difficult for those who haven't lost a spouse. The fact is, we've all experienced or will experience loss on some level.

Death is part of the nature of life. Each time we experience loss and grief, our grief journey takes us down a different path. Just because our path is different from someone else's path doesn't mean that we can't connect with them or that we can't understand their journey. Sometimes the widowed feel ashamed that they're grieving so much or that their grief prevents them from doing some of the things they used to do. Invite them to tell their story. They're probably holding back because they think you don't want to hear it. An invitation can go a long way and help them find meaningful connections and further their sense of belonging. By sharing our stories we can save a life and make a difference in someone's life. And yes, it is also a way to let them know that it's okay to talk about loss — about death and the effects of its aftermath to the loved ones who are left behind.

One of the things that surprised me most as I began my grief journey was the number of things I would have to grieve. I knew I'd have to grieve my husband, but I didn't realize that so many things that I loved in life were tied to the man I loved. Now I have to grieve those too. It seems like every day I stumble across something that I lost — something that was part of the life I had with him but has now vanished. That loss makes me angry. I find myself raging against what is because it is not what I think it should be. I get so tired of seeing empty spaces that used to be filled with joy. My connection to him connected me to so many things about myself that I learned to love over time. It's that connection to myself that I have to embrace now. I have to learn to see and discover those things about myself that used to be so easy for him to see. I have to learn to belong to myself again and love who I am at my core.

It's not always easy to accept belonging to oneself — to know yourself. There are days when I go within and simply sit at the curb with my anger or my sadness. One of the biggest things I've had to learn is to have compassion for myself. It has always been so easy for me to be compassionate towards others, but I rarely saved any of that for myself. Learning self-compassion was one of my biggest grieving lessons. Of course, I haven't thoroughly learned it. I still struggle. My expectations of myself are high and at times it's hard to let them go.

Resilience isn't bouncing back right away. Sometimes it's being strong enough to hold on for a while until you are ready to do the bouncing. When we suffer something like loss, we're not going to heal from it and bounce back right away. After three years, there are parts of me that are still recovering. There are challenges that I've carried with me along the way that I'm only just now addressing. Belonging isn't easy. I know it takes work on my part, and it takes a welcoming acceptance on the part of others. Those two things have to align, and there are no guarantees that they will. Will I find or create a tribe? I can't tell you, but I can tell you I'm working on getting back to my baseline. Resilience is getting back to that baseline and realizing that I belong to me. I belong to myself and that will be enough no matter what is stacked in front of me.

10

Resilience Isn't Perfect

When you lose someone, everyone wants you to be okay but on their timeline. Unless others have stood where you stand, they have no idea that the emotional terror you're feeling is so much worse than they can imagine. Despite your best efforts at grace, deep inside you feel like you're standing in the crater of what was once your life and often standing on your knees. People will lay baskets of advice at your feet and will try to measure your resilience by how much of your life you try to get back. None of that is helpful. What they don't see is that the most powerful thing they can do is to bear witness to the fact that your life has been destroyed and stand beside you. You will realize your resilience, starting with the desire to wake up and take a breath every day. Your resilience, amid so much darkness and chaos, is simply that you are enough.

Being enough is a sentiment that is echoed throughout much of my writing. It is an idea that I embrace and that I love to share. The idea that we're not enough permeates our modern society. We find ourselves making that idea a part of who we are without even noticing it. It's no different when it comes to grief. One of the things I've noticed about the prolific grief industry is that everyone wants to sell you their idea of coping with grief and loss. The implied message is that you aren't enough and won't know how to deal with your grief. Usually, because they've been through a grief journey of their own, and they think they know best and have the answers you need. There is a guide for you on every corner, and everyone will be offering you a blueprint for how to "move on" or to "move forward."

I've grown to loathe the sentiment that we don't move on from grief, but we move forward with it. Forward assumes we're still headed in the same direction and that all the same goals apply. It bypasses the fact that our lives have been irrevocably changed. The rebuilding of our lives may not suit others' expectations. Resilience isn't achieving some bright, shiny new life that others are expecting. Resilience can also be having just enough strength to make it to the next day. People will keep wondering why you're not making faster progress when all you're doing is trying to tread water carefully in an unfamiliar sea.

The average human can tread water for approximately 3 hours. A skilled athlete can make it 8, depending on the weather. Just thinking about treading water in an open sea is exhausting. Grief is exhausting, standing still is exhausting, and taking a step in any direction is exhausting. The state of being exhausted is exhausting. As I approach the end of my third year on my grief journey, I am exhausted.

I'm often told that things will get better. Perhaps that is what people feel like they're supposed to say. Maybe some even honestly believe it. The truth is that no one can know if things will get better for you or not. As much as I'd like to cling to the great lie of "it gets better," the water still gets harder to tread, and waves still get higher. I'm reminded that some hurricanes have sustained themselves for over four weeks. Storms aren't guaranteed to end when we want them to end. People take great joy in telling us the storm will pass because it makes them seem experienced and wise. Even if we know the storm will die out, we can become weary from just being in the storm for so long. I don't want to hear that the storm will pass, but I want to know that you see me in the storm and that you've stretched out your hand to help in some meaningful way. I hope that you'll give me respite from the storm so that I can regain my energy to tread the water again. People love to toss around the idea of moving forward, but forward is relative in the swells of a stormy and endless ocean. Only those of us in the throes of grief can decide the direction we will go and whether or not we'll deem that direction forward.

I keep treading. Isn't that what being resilient is all about? It's the ability to return to a state of normalcy after difficulty. Despite those who would sell you on the idea that it means having a shiny new life after the trauma of loss, none of that is guaranteed. Any shiny newness is simply luck. After Jayson died, I received all sorts of random emails and social media shares. People wanted to show me a clip they had seen or share with me a story they had read about someone who "overcame" their grief. Invariably these stories were about someone who'd lost a spouse, but now they had moved forward and I could too if I just followed their road map. Most of them had remarried and had created new families. Many of them had started new businesses that were wildly successful. The message was always the same. I could choose to do the same thing. I could have a bright, shiny new life that was even more spectacular than the life I had before.

There was only one problem. I liked the life I had before. I'm not sure that I can recreate that life or any reasonable facsimile of it. Of course, I know I can't have what I had with Jayson because that was the alchemy of the two of us combined. I often feel like I am the oil to the water of life. The hope I was being pitched felt cheap and plastic. There was still much I had to mourn.

I tried fighting against the messages that bombarded me daily, but it was to no avail. "You'll get there," people kept saying. As if my arrival at their idea of hope and resilience was inevitable. I still needed to sit with what I was losing. I had worked my entire life to get to this point. All of my plans, all of my dreams, all of my hopes were unfolding in ways that I had always wanted. Then in the span of just over a year, they were gone — all of them. I had to reset, and no video of some thirty-something person who had a new life was going to help me do that.

Normalcy is a baseline, and one could argue that resiliency is a return to that baseline. To have expectations otherwise is to set yourself up for disappointment. That's what I felt like everyone was doing — setting me up for disappointment. No one can know the outcome of any gamble. I still don't know how my career is going to turn out. The videos I was sent would suggest that it would be wildly successful because that's how grief works. The realist in me thinks it will be successful if I apply the right skill to it. In the end this might not be the case, as my resilience doesn't depend on whether or not I'm a good entrepreneur. My resilience is being able to try something else if that doesn't work.

If you listen to what others expect your resilience to be for long enough, you start to believe that's what you should be achieving. Then, when you don't reach some sort of success right away, the disappointment begins to set in. There have been many days when I thought I wasn't doing it right because I hadn't hit the success I thought I was supposed to. Shame starts to creep in, and you have to wonder if something is wrong with you because you don't have this shiny new life that everyone holds out as successful resilience. There is nothing worse than to think that you're failing at grief. Because of the high expectations I have of myself, I already feel like a failure on so many levels.

There is not a day that goes by that I don't feel like a failure as a parent. I work hard to be sure my children always have a good meal in front of them, that they take a nutritious lunch to school, that they have clean clothes, that they're bathed, well-rested, and happy. That's a tall order for a person who is also trying to be a good provider. As any parent knows, children also come with various appointments, play dates, extracurricular activities, and school events. They need help with homework, tutoring for subjects when they get behind and someone to listen to all the stories of what happens at school. Two-parent families usually tag team these activities —at least we did. But now, with two children depending on just me, I feel like there isn't enough of me to go around. I feel like I let them down every day and that they deserve better. I hope that they will look back on this time with me with more grace than I have for myself, and realize that I was doing the very best I could for them. I hope they know that I would carry the world on my shoulders for them.

Sometimes hope feels like an unattainable expectation that's forced upon you. The more people talked to me about how much better things would get, the more ashamed I became that I wasn't doing it all. My business wasn't off to a wildly successful start, and there certainly wasn't going to be any new romance. Try as I might, I couldn't lose the grief weight I had gained from eating my feelings. I was too exhausted to exercise or do anything for myself at the end of what were becoming very long days. All of this was compounded by the pandemic that was sweeping the globe at the time. Every day became a repeat of the last and another day that I didn't achieve enough of what I felt like I was supposed to achieve.

"One day, it will get better," they said. "One day, you'll look back on all of this and realize how far you've come," they said. One day feels so far off. It's a future I still can't see. As of this writing, it has been 1,095 days since Jayson died. As I look across those days, I don't feel like I've come very far at all. There is so much about this feeling of loss and grief that hasn't at all changed. Indeed, I've gone through iterations of how I will work and how I'll make a living.

I've even thought about selling the house and downsizing. But some shifts in the local market made waiting a better option. I do wonder if I could have done it if the market was right. Would it have opened new doors for me mentally, or would I feel like I had just gone down another new path for which I don't care? I still have a hard time with letting some things go. I boxed up some of Jayson's sweaters when I was staging the house. They are still in the garage — ready for donation. The closet still essentially looks like it did when he died. I haven't moved his clothes or his shoes. I know that he's not coming back, but I still find the letting go difficult. Maybe I'm afraid of the finality of it all, if I clear out his things. Maybe I'm afraid I'll forget him, if I don't see his clothes hanging in front of me every morning. I'm quite sure my delay doesn't fit some timeline I'm supposed to follow.

People close to me often hear me say how much I hate this new life. That sentiment is largely true. After all, I keep comparing it to the life I had, and it's not nearly as good. I know I shouldn't do that. The old life is gone, and I won't be getting it back. But this new life is so full of struggle. I had hoped that struggle would only be during the first year as I adjusted to a life without him in it. But, the struggles continue. Every day there are the routine struggles of parenting and keeping a house. Then there are the struggles of trying to move my business forward. I wish I could say that things get easier, but they just don't — or at least they haven't for me. But I still get up. I still face each day. I still look for some break in the struggle. I look for some ray of sun through the ever-present storm clouds. I am still here.

If resilience isn't the snake oil they're selling me with the shiny new life and the shiny new family, what is it? I've learned that I have to move on from the shame and disappointment I am feeling by holding myself up to someone else's standards. I have to figure out what my resilience looks like. I need to know to what baseline I am returning. I have to take a step back and take a look at everything that has happened in my life over the last 1,095 days and see the bigger picture. I have to figure out how to give myself some grace. That, for me, isn't always easy to do. I tend to prefer to beat myself up instead. I wish I could say that I know exactly what I want and which direction my life will go. But I don't. No idea and no direction have really gained any traction. I'm still sad more often than not. I miss my old life and I miss my husband.

Taking that approach, I've realized that resilience is far simpler than what everyone keeps making it out to be. What I am bouncing back to is a place of gratefulness and of hope. I lost everything and that created a surge of bitterness and anger in me. In wildly spinning through life trying to quickly recreate something that was as good or reminiscent of what I had, I was exhausting myself and hurtling headlong into disappointment. I have realized that life doesn't have to be something shiny and new, and I certainly don't have to create any sort of new and amazing life out of what I have been given. My first step is simply allowing myself to feel cheated and sit with the defeat I have been handed. That is no easy task when you have a family depending on you, but it is a necessary one. If there is a God, he had abandoned me in my darkest hour, and he has not returned. I have to accept where I am so that I can figure out where I go next.

So many people keep pushing positivity at me, and that feels toxic. While I definitely believe in the idea of having a positive mindset, I also think that we need to acknowledge and allow our feelings to surface. Sadness, anger, and even disappointment are all human emotions. We feel these things for a reason, and to be told that we should keep a positive outlook without feeling our emotions, or stuffing them down, only creates emotional damage. It's unhealthy to repress our emotions. Ignoring them can have a negative ripple effect in every aspect of our lives, especially our health and our relationships with those closest to us. These emotions aren't inherently wrong. They are just inherently human. To judge them, or to judge ourselves, puts unnecessary pressure on us to rush through them and to feel instead those emotions that society deems more positive.

There are some days when I'm despondent, and why shouldn't I be? My husband was an amazing man, and he's not here anymore. I miss him not only because of my relationship with him but also because of the father he was to our daughters and the man he was to so many others. The fact that he is gone is sad, but if I allow myself to experience that sadness, then I can move through it just as I'm supposed to. The sadness reminds me of the depth of love that I had for him.

There are certainly days that I am angry. I feel slighted because I wanted to have a longer time with him. My daughters should have gotten to grow up with their Daddy. Anger is probably the more difficult emotion to allow and with which to sit. Anger tends to want to be directed, and for a man with a broken faith, that anger often gets directed at the "God" he was promised would answer prayers. I get angry that the expected miracle never came. But anger is essential because to feel it is to understand it. Knowing what drives my anger helps me understand my fear and allows me to accept and transition from what is. More simply, anger has its purpose. It can be our best friend during the most trying times of our lives and a positive, driving force behind our survival.

The most important thing that I have discovered on my journey is the power of gratefulness. Indeed, there are plenty of things for which I am not grateful. It's very easy to get a victim mentality and focus on the fact that all of these things have happened to me. In reality, they are things that have just happened. That is so much easier to write than to do. I remind myself daily that I have two beautiful daughters for whom I'm grateful. They are funny, intelligent, beautiful, and annoying all at the same time. When I'm so frustrated that I hate being a parent, I can usually find my way back to all the reasons I love being their father.

My gratefulness also extends to my family. No matter what, their love has been constant. Through all of the ups and downs of my life, they have been there — on the front row, ready to cheer, catch me, and even weep with me. Jayson extended that family. I had the good fortune to inherit his family too. They have continued with me, grieving in their way, but never failing to show me love and kindness. Sometimes, that feeds my anger as well. Why does he have to miss out on sharing so much goodness and love? The whole thing doesn't seem fair. Truthfully, the anger stems from the fact that I was cheated out of sharing all of it with him.

Jayson always inspired me to be my best self. He stuck by me through hard times, called me out when I got lost in my negativity or became self-destructive. He stuck by me through thick and thin and everything in between. Now it's all up to me. Oddly, or not so oddly, he knew it would be.

He knew I planned and executed against a master plan. So he made me make promises. There were the financial promises. Those weren't so hard. I'd always followed his financial advice. Then there were his wishes for the girls. Those promises are so easy. He'd always taken such loving care of them. Then there were the promises that concerned me. Those are not so easy, and that's probably why he made me make them. He knew I'd revert to walling myself off if he were gone. He knew that I'd allow grief to consume me to the point that I'd never look outward — unless I promised him I'd do so.

Losing Jayson is much like standing on a mountain. It's like standing on a lush, green, flower-covered mountain. Then suddenly, without warning, the peak is blown off and changed into an erupting caldera. Lava pours down and engulfs everything in its path. You're frozen and unable to move. The searing pain swirls around you, and all you can do is cry. And in the aftermath, when all that's left is the rumble under the mountain and ash falling from the sky, everything that you've known and loved is gone. Life is in pieces.

So many well-meaning people offer guidance and advice. None of it ever really rings true, even if they've experienced the same eruption on their mountain. After all, we all love in unique and individual ways, and so too is our grief unique and personal. For a time, we have to sit alone on the ash-covered mountain. We sit alone and we weep. We could use the mud from our tears to begin to build walls to protect ourselves. I know that every brick laid is a broken promise. If there was one thing my husband knew — it was joy. Joy doesn't come from walls.

Sometimes I just sit in the mud, refraining from making bricks and pondering how I'll keep my promises. The least I can do is what the most spectacular man I have ever known asked of me.

He asked that I be open. He asked that I be vulnerable. He asked that I let life find me. Wherever I ended up, let it find me and bring me joy again. It was so much easier to say yes when I thought we had more time. This big life is bigger because grief has moved in. But now I know I have to save a seat for joy, and the two of them have to sit together.

Until then, I sit on this mountain of ash. I watch the clouds come and go, and the rain of my tears fall into the ash. But peeking through, there is the smallest sprout appearing from the ash. It's the sprout from the seed of joy he left me, and it is a flower called hope. The thing is, it's my hope and it's exactly how I've defined it for myself. I have learned that we should never let anyone else define hope for us. What others tend to do is give us their idea of what hope is, and we are then expected to embrace that hope. Your hope is your own.

Healing involves storytelling. When we share our story, we're not only opening the pathways for our own healing, but we also help others heal. I've given you my story, but how many other stories are out there? I encourage you to seek them out and listen to them. My grief will not be your grief. My path to healing will not be your path. Sure, some bits and pieces of my journey have probably rung true for you. Take those things and do what you need with them. But listening to others tell their story allows them to heal and lets you see the infinite number of options for healing and traveling through your own grief journey.

The future will happen regardless of us. There are days that I just want to sit and let time pass. I refuse to feel guilty for that. Taking the time and sitting with whatever emotions I have is as important as actively engaging in a task or pursuing a goal. Sometimes, I just want to see how certain things are going to play out. Rushing it or pushing it along won't always change the outcome for the better.

Right now, I don't have a long-term plan. I used to hate the interview questions that ask, "Where do you see yourself in five years?" I have no idea. My focus is on where I see myself in the morning. My focus is on making it out of bed and to the shower. Some would think I should have moved farther along in almost three years, but here I am. I'm learning to have the grace to let myself simply be in this place.

Three years is 1,095 days. That's how long I've lived without him. It seems impossible that I have made it this long, but yet I have. At no point did it get any easier like I was told it would. The pain of missing him is persistent and sharp. I was told it would come in waves, but it has been steady and unrelenting, and I find myself always just under the surface. I can still remember my walk out of his hospital room, the wailing in the car as I left the parking garage, and the desire to rip the universe entirely in two. All of those emotions and feelings are still there and don't seem to be going anywhere. The challenge for me has been figuring out how to live with them. I do wonder what the next 1,095 days will bring. I would like to say that my business will be a raging success, but it might not. I've got to figure out the right balance of being a parent and a provider, which is in and of itself a moving target.

I have walked away from the idea of dating. Whether I'm ready or not, letting go of that has been healthy. This last chapter is about me and not about me with someone else. It is certainly not about someone else's idea of what my life should look like. My children need me to be present every day, and I have to be sure that I can give them everything they deserve so that their start in life is a good one. There is plenty to keep me busy.

On the bookshelf behind my desk is a copy of Emily Post's _Etiquette_. I believe in doing things in the most proper and gracious way possible. Grace, after all, is the ability to make others feel comfortable with you. But there is no way to feel comfortable in grief. It's a solitary journey. No one can go on that journey with you, and there is no right way to do grief. Just as our fingerprints are different, we all grieve differently, and no one can tell us how to do it. We cannot invite others into our grieving, but they can bear witness. There is no proper way to grieve, unlike the kind thank you note or the gracious nod to the proper fork.

Time has no healing power. To wait for it to work some magic is futile. The mind may soften painful memories or make joyful ones more pronounced, but the memory of trauma is embedded not only into our minds, but into our bodies as well. As we go through our day-to-day, even the smallest of movements can recall the pain that lies just beneath the surface — the constant pain that doesn't ebb and flow, but is sharp, consistent, and now part of who we are.

When we lose someone to whom we're connected, we never get over that — despite the wishes or best intentions of those around us. People waiting for us to "bounce back" set expectations in their mind for what our resilience will look like. We have to be careful that we don't adopt those expectations as our own. Just getting up, taking that next breath, and choosing to live another day all while learning how to manage the chronic pain of loss is resilience.

When we grieve, we like to think our pain is unique or that no one has suffered as we suffer. I have learned that I am not alone in grief. Social media continually shows me friends who have drifted in and out of my life; their unbridled joy and exquisite pain are all laid bare. None of us were ever any better than or not as good as the other. Life is inescapable.

Every day I'm reminded that I made it to another day, and that's enough. Every day that I don't go under in this crazy endless ocean is another day of resilience. Walking on water was so much easier when there was someone there to catch me. Now, every step is unsure. Only I can decide what I'll do with each day that is before me. There is no guide or directive for how to navigate this, even though we all wish there were. I learn something new as each day goes by, and I share the story of my journey in hopes that some small part may help someone else. I can't walk with you on your path and you can't walk with me on mine, but I know your pain. I see it. I'm your witness.

I'm also reminded I have to continue to learn to accept and be open each day. Accepting adds peace to my resilience. Surviving with peace reminds me that I am enough. I encourage you to find your own story. Sit with it, and then prepare to tell it. It's your story, after all. It doesn't matter if it doesn't fit with someone else's idea of what healing is supposed to look like. Your hope is your own and it's inside of you. Every time you tell your story, you'll be one step closer to healing.

What I have found on my journey is to let go of the shame. I have learned to ask for help when I need it and to build communities on my terms. It's important to seek out a licensed therapist if you need it. None of this journey has to be what someone else tells you it should be. You are resilient enough just to carry this burden until you've decided which way is forward and how you want to process it on your terms. You just need to look inside yourself for your resilience, embrace your feelings, and accept that you are enough. Remember, this is your journey!

CPSIA information can be obtained
at www.ICGtesting.com
Printed in the USA
BVHW040838230222
629871BV00015B/500

9 781957 013114